What readers say about
Bumps in the Road

I really enjoyed the history of this book - definitely worth reading. The true adventure of this family was completely amazing.

_____T. Brand

* * * * * *

I loved this book...hope she writes more...thanks:))

_____Ginny

* * * * * *

This is delightful. Rose has a marvelous way of describing things and proves that truth is much better than fiction. I loved her remarks on ham radio. The life she lived at the mine was amazing. I could not have done it. I admire her very much. The book is excellent.

_____Virginia

* * * * * *

Rose will entertain you while sharing the experiences that have made her one of the most well informed and excellent writers about Alaska. Buy her book, it will be a big hit with the entire family.

_____Rosalyn Stowell

* * * * * *

Excellent - I loved it - Read it in one day, could not put it down.

_____Bill Quailes

BUMPS

----IN THE----

ROAD

SECOND EDITION

PUBLISHED BY:

MAMMOTH ENTERPRISE, GEMALASKA
1023 8TH Avenue
Fairbanks, AK 99701

LARGE PRINT

ROSE RYBACHEK

BUMPS

----IN THE----

ROAD

SECOND EDITION

My Family's
(Mis)Adventures along
Alaska's Elliott Highway,
1959-1980

Bumps in the Road, My Family's (Mis)Adventures along Alaska's Elliott Highway, 1959-1980, 2nd Edition. Fairbanks, AK

Copyright 2015 by Rose Rybachek

Published in the United States of America by Mammoth Enterprises, Gemalaska, 1023 8th Avenue, Fairbanks, Alaska 99701

ISBN: 0692945938
ISBN: 9780692945933

The Library of Congress has established a Catalog-in-publications record for this title.

Library of Congress Control Number: 2015916972

This large print edition published in accordance with the standards of the N.A.V.H.

Other books by this Author:
Mining for Alaskan Adventures Volume I, 2017
Mining for Alaskan Adventures Volume II, 2017

TABLE OF CONTENTS

DEDICATION

While I may have portrayed my late husband, Stan, as a bit reckless in this book, he was a very capable person, and able to find a solution to every problem. He made my whole life an adventure, and I dedicate *Bumps in the Road, 2nd Edition* to him. I also dedicate *Bumps in the Road, 2nd Edition* to the memory of my son Danny; my Mom; my Dad; and my sister Betty; who have all left this earth for a better place. And finally, I wish to thank our three daughters, Sue, Sallie, and Cyndi. Their support and assistance has been invaluable. Without their assistance, there would not have been *Bumps in the Road, 2nd Edition.*

INTRODUCTION

Thanks to the U. S. Air Force, Stan and I moved to Alaska in September 1958. Stan (my husband of a little over a year), was to report for duty on October 1, 1958 on Ladd Air Force Base located adjacent to Fairbanks. Alaska was still a Territory at the time we arrived, officially becoming a State on January 1, 1959. Since I was about six months pregnant, the Air Force would not authorize me to travel the Alcan Highway, saying that I should fly to Alaska after Stan had established a residence. However, being slightly rebellious, we decided to drive anyway.

My Dad had always dreamed of going to Alaska, and this seemed like an answer to his dreams. After a little persuasion, my parents decided to travel with us. Stan, my Dad, my Mom, my two sisters, my brother, and I, along with two dogs and two cats, arrived in Fairbanks on September 27, 1958. That trip is another story.

Stan soon became friends with two old-time Sourdoughs, John and Tony Radak, in the town of Livengood, eighty-four miles from where we settled in the North Pole area. He spent innumerable hours visiting with them, cutting wood for them, hauling gas and groceries to them, and just being a Good Samaritan. The saying was that the definition of a sourdough was "sour on Alaska, but not enough dough to leave." However, I believe the official definition of a sourdough was someone that had been in Alaska for a long time.

My parents and siblings stayed in Alaska for nearly five years, until my Dad frosted his lungs in December 1962, cranking on a bulldozer to start it at minus 40°F. He moved the family back to Montana the following July. Stan's enlistment in the Air Force was up in June of that same year, 1963.

Meanwhile in 1961, Stan had negotiated with one of the old timers (John) for some gold mining claims on Wilbur Creek. He soon had my Dad involved, since my Dad had been a coal miner in Montana for years. The claims were approximately ten miles from the town of Livengood. In June of 1963, after Stan's discharge from the Air Force, we moved the family to a cabin on the mining claims. By that time, our family consisted of Danny, age four; Sue, age two; and Sallie age one.

During the early years of its existence, the Elliott Highway was closed between Fairbanks and Livengood when the Powers that Be suspected that winter weather was on its way. This closure normally occurred around the middle of September. With the road closed, we needed to do substantial planning for the supplies that we would need to lay in for the winter. We could potentially be snowed-in for around five months. Ever try to keep eggs edible for five months? It can be done.

We spent three summers and two winters at the cabin before we moved back to the North Pole area in 1965. We considered teaching our kids using the correspondence course that the State of Alaska provided, but decided the kids needed to learn how to interact with other kids. Danny, our oldest, was enrolled in first grade, and Sue was enrolled in kindergarten.

We continued to work to develop the mining property, spending weekends and vacations at the mine, but living during the winter at our place in North Pole. We made many trips up and down the Elliott Highway, which is also the first leg of the road to the North Slope recently made famous by the TV show, *Ice Road Truckers*.

* * * * * * *

I think my fascination with the Elliott Highway began the first time we drove over it to Livengood during the summer of 1959. It was a narrow, winding, gravel and dirt road that wended its way through stately groves of birch trees; past scraggly spruce; over barren hills with magnificent views; past huge rocks; over several picturesque rivers; and through blueberry fields. We were lucky in spotting several moose browsing as we drove along. Stan had been over the road many times before he offered to let me come with him. He was an experienced tour guide, and pointed out some interesting aspects of the countryside along the Highway.

According to John and Tony, when they first came to Livengood shortly after the gold strike in 1914, there was no road access. Supplies were barged up the Yukon River, then up the Tolovana River to a huge, dirt covered log-jam on the West Fork of the Tolovana River. From there they had a rail system using dray horses to pull railroad cars to the other side of the log jam. Then, the supplies would be loaded into wagons drawn by teams of horses, and hauled into the town of Livengood. No wonder an egg could cost a dollar or more!

They said that later an overland trail had been constructed, but due to the mountainous terrain, and inclement weather, it was only passable during the winter months.

John and Tony told us that during WWII, the army had upgraded the winter trail, and put in some Bailey Bridges across several of the more problematic creeks and rivers. (I never quite figured out what a "Bailey Bridge" was, but I believe it to have been a prefabricated truss bridge made from wood and steel, and light enough that they didn't require a crane for installation.)

The army used this trail to supply its posts further north. They called this winter trail the Green Lightning Road. When the war was over, the Army destroyed or removed most of the Bailey Bridges, so the town was again without a useful road.

In the late 1950s, the Territory of Alaska began work on a year-around road that was planned to extend to Nome. It reached Livengood in 1957. They named this road the Elliott Highway, in honor of Malcom Elliott. Mr. Elliott was president of the Alaska Road Commission between 1927 and 1932. Each summer, the Territory would add more miles to the existing road. By 1959, the road had reached Manley Hot Springs, nearly ninety miles northwest of Livengood. However, with the advent of Statehood effective January 1, 1959, the State apparently had better use for its money, so the road went just a bit further than Manley Hot Springs, to Tofty, and the project was shelved.

We made many trips up and down the Elliott Highway. Sometimes we ventured beyond the town of Livengood, but mostly we only traveled as far as the town. Livengood was located at approximately 69 Mile on the Elliott and was nearly a ghost town when we first visited. The Elliott Highway begins at Fox, which is about twelve miles north of Fairbanks. North Pole is another twelve miles to the south of Fairbanks. My family experienced many adventures along the scenic Elliott Highway.

When you read the following stories, you'll find that Danny figured prominently in them until the year 1967. We lost him that summer in a drowning accident.

The following stories are based upon our (mis)adventures along the Elliott Highway.

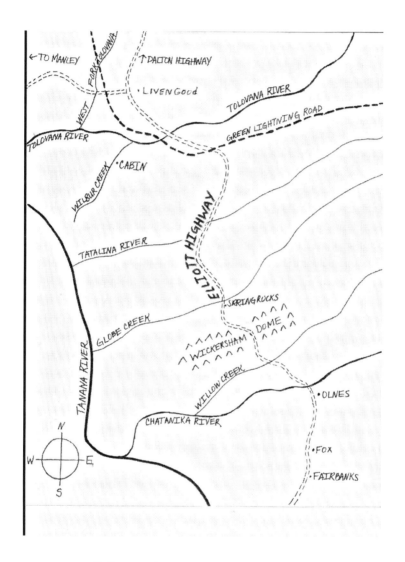

Map of Elliott Highway

Chapter 1

Round is Better than Wishbone

"Why don't we go hunting?" Stan asked me one bright, sunny morning in February 1959. "I don't have to work today, and it looks like a perfect day to see if we can find some bunnies."

"It does look like a wonderful day to be out and about," I replied. "I'll ask Mom if she would mind watching Danny this afternoon, and we can go." Danny, our first born, was only two months old.

"Okay and I'll find out if we can borrow your Dad's Jeep."

My parents, three siblings, Stan, Danny and I were all sharing the same house in Fairbanks, waiting for summer when each family would get a separate house. But, for our purposes that day, the arrangement was perfect. Mom agreed with no hesitation to watch Danny, and Dad told us to go ahead and use the Jeep.

Stan and I got ready to go. We packed our .22 rifles, snowshoes, parkas, gloves, boots, and a small lunch. It wasn't long before we were on our way.

Since we had arrived in the Fairbanks area in September 1958, Stan had been exploring the countryside. He was the "expert" on the area, and he decided that the area near the Chatanika River would be a good place to look for bunnies. Since the highway department had closed the Elliott Highway just a few miles past the Chatanika River for the winter, he thought there would be little or no traffic – and he was right.

As we drove along, I said, "Stan, you know I have never been on snowshoes in my life. What if I break my neck?"

"Don't worry," he said with a chuckle. "It's much easier than downhill skiing!" This comment didn't offer me very much comfort. About two weeks before this, we had decided to go downhill skiing at the Resort on Ladd Air Force Base (now Fort Wainwright). I had previously only done some cross-country skiing. They had an interesting-looking tow-rope to haul you to the top of the hill. All you had to do was get in line, grab onto the rope when it was your turn, and you'd soon be at the top of the slope. I planned to drop off about halfway up the slope, since this was my first experience with downhill skiing. Stan forgot to tell me that when you grabbed the rope, you were supposed to glide forward on your skis. I grabbed the rope, and my feet stuck right where they were. I stretched out to what felt like twelve feet long before I had sense enough to turn loose of the tow-rope. Instead of being kind and understanding he had the unmitigated gall to laugh so hard he was crying. So, with that recent experience in mind, do you think his reference to downhill skiing set my mind at ease?

Besides, we had been married for a year and a half and I had found, much to my chagrin, every time Stan told me not to worry, something bad would happen.

We had an uneventful trip to the Chatanika River; it wasn't long before we were at a fairly wide spot in the road, where we could safely leave the Jeep. There were tracks of wild animals: moose, rabbit, wolf, fox and lynx on the river and in the vegetation growing beside it.

Donning the snowshoes was no easy feat. They were shaped kind of like a wishbone, with webbing in between the arms. Once you got your feet strapped into the contraption, you had to waddle like a duck with your feet apart to keep from stepping on your other snowshoe. I finally figured that out after taking several tumbles into the snow caused by stepping on one snowshoe or the other. Once you were down in the deep snow it took a mighty effort to get upright.

Before long, I had the hang of it, and we were making pretty good time down the trail toward the Chatanika River. "How are you doing?" Stan called back over his shoulder.

"Just fine," I replied. "I'm nearly keeping up with you."

"I think we'd better split up along the banks of the river. That way, we'll probably have a better chance of seeing a bunny. If you see one, just whistle, and he'll stop to look at you, and you can shoot him."

"How do I keep from getting lost?" I asked.

"If you get lost, you can always follow your tracks back to the road. Don't worry, it will be fun." And with that, he turned and took off down what appeared to be nothing but a rabbit trail. I, on the other hand, did worry.

I kept to the trail for a while, but since I had finally mastered those snowshoes, I decided that I, too, could be brave and venture off the trail into the willows. I made my way down the very next bunny trail I found. Things were going well, until there was a little twig sticking up that I hadn't seen. It managed to get hooked into the corner of the wye in my snowshoe, and when I tried to pick up that foot, it wouldn't move. Of course, since I was off-balance with my foot tethered to the twig, down I went. My gun barrel jammed into the snow, and there I was in a most ungainly heap.

I figured the first thing I should do was to clean the snow out of the barrel of my gun. I'd heard horror stories about people shooting a gun with the barrel jammed full of snow, so I broke off another twig, and managed to get most of the snow out of the barrel. I still hadn't realized what tripped me, so I tried to get back to my feet on the snowshoes. Finally managing to stand upright, I tried another step, with the same dire consequences. Down I went again, and again the gun barrel jammed into the snow.

By this time, I was becoming an expert at cleaning it out. I was wriggling and writhing around in the snow, looking for a suitable twig, when I sensed something. There, standing on the trail looking at me, was the biggest bunny I had ever seen. He was apparently trying to puzzle out what was on his trail. He probably had never seen a human being before, at least not flopping around in the snow.

About that time, I heard Stan yell, "There's a moose over here, be careful!"

When Stan yelled, the bunny leaped forward. He was charging right at me, and I was in no position to shoot him, since I still had snow in my gun barrel. I desperately started whistling, but instead of stopping, the bunny came faster. I was truly happy when he veered away at the last minute, and I wasn't run over by that rampaging bunny.

However, by this time, I could hear the crunch in the snow of the approaching moose. I still couldn't do anything but lie there helplessly as the moose approached. I wondered, *would a whistle stop a moose?* It certainly hadn't done much for the bunny, but it was worth a shot.

Whistling madly, I scrambled around trying to free both my gun and my snowshoe. By this time, I had figured out what the problem was with the snowshoe, but when you are stretched out full length in the snow, it is hard to get your left foot free from a twig. Finally, with a sigh of relief, I managed to free my foot, and get to my feet. The moose passed within ten feet of me, but didn't appear interested in me at all. I was quite happy about that.

When I was finally upright and ready to go again, I yelled at Stan that I was going back to the Jeep. I was finished hunting for a while. He decided that it was probably time to go, too. It was a comforting sight to see the Jeep patiently waiting for us.

That was the last time I ever tried to use snowshoes of that kind. From then on, I used the round ones. It is much harder to catch them on a twig.

Our first home in Fairbanks located in Island Homes
subdivision

Chapter 2

Too Big to Straddle

By the time August rolled around in 1959, Stan had accrued a whole month of leave time. He had become good friends with John and Tony, and was concerned that they might not have a sufficient wood supply to see them through the winter.

Both John and Tony were in their eighties and wood cutting was becoming more and more difficult for them. At least that was Stan's thought. August was also the month that moose season opened.

One morning, Stan said to me, "I want to go moose hunting and woodcutting for the month. Any objections?"

"When do you want to go?" I replied. I guess Danny and I would be fine while you are gone."

"I think I should leave here on August 20, and come back on September 20," he replied.

I agreed that this would be a meaningful project, and besides, it would give him a worthwhile outlet for burning off some of his excess energy. He asked my Dad if he could borrow the Jeep and trailer, and Dad was willing.

Stan packed his gear and left the evening of August 19. He planned to set up camp on the West Fork of the Tolovana River. I heard nothing from him for a couple of weeks. One evening I heard the Jeep motor in the driveway. He was home! I raced to the door, flung it open, and yelled, "Did you get a moose?"

"No," he said. "I ran out of coffee, so decided to come home. A hot shower would feel awfully good right about now."

I had been so excited that I hadn't noticed he was a bit "gamey". He enjoyed his hot shower, and then he surprised me. "How would you like to come with me for the rest of my leave?" he asked. "It gets mighty lonely up there by the West Fork, especially at night."

I was more than willing. Mom was an eager babysitter, so bright and early the next morning we gathered Danny's belongings and took him to her house. We then got our supplies ready, and off we went for my very first moose hunting trip.

Stan had followed his plans, and set up his tent near the West Fork. With the additional supplies we brought (mostly coffee, but also a full barrel of gas), we figured we could spend the rest of his leave time (about ten days) camped there with no problem. It was Stan's practice to get up every morning before daylight, build a fire, make coffee, and go hunting by driving up and down the roads.

Road hunting for big game was quite a new experience for me. The only hunting I had previously done was in Montana, where we would find a spot to sit and wait for deer to pass. I was quite excited that first morning to hear Stan stirring in the dark, but I was not quite so excited when I heard him yell, "Come on, sleepy-head, time to rise and shine."

"Do I have to get out of my nice warm sleeping bag?" I asked. "Can't you just deliver me some coffee? It smells so good."

"Get out of that bag before I dump you out," he replied.

Knowing him like I did, I knew that he wasn't shy about carrying out his threats, so I crawled out of the sleeping bag and got myself dressed in warm clothes. Before long, we were on that long road, keeping our eyes peeled for any game we might find.

"Look," I hollered about ten minutes after we had left our campsite. "Isn't that a grouse sitting there by the side of the road?"

"It sure looks like one," Stan said. "Grouse would make a great dinner meat for tonight's dinner."

With that, he pulled over to the side of the road, got out his .22 rifle, and soon the grouse was in the back of the jeep. He was right, it was very tasty that night.

We continued Stan's practice of hunting in the early morning, cutting wood for the old-timers during the middle of the day, delivering it, and then hunting in the evening. They were full days.

We did this until it was time to return to Fairbanks. And as we packed up our camp and got ready to make the drive we were torn between wanting to get hugs from Danny and just staying forever in our snug camping spot.

However, duty called, and we did have to leave. We got everything loaded and were driving along with our nearly empty gas barrel tied in the trailer, when I spotted what looked like a huge sink hole getting bigger and bigger on the right side of the road. I wondered *why doesn't Stan slow down or go around it?* In the blink of an eye we hit that sink hole, and we both nearly went through the roof of the Jeep. Our gas barrel flew out of the trailer like it had been fired from a cannon. It ended up across the ditch.

"Why didn't you slow down?" I hollered at Stan. Meanwhile, I tried to get my neck back into joint by stretching and rubbing the top of my head where it had hit the roof.

"I thought I could straddle that darned hole," Stan replied. "And when I realized that I couldn't, it was too late to do anything but hit it. If I'd tried to turn then, we would have flipped over when only one wheel dropped down in it."

We managed to retrieve our barrel and get it back in the trailer. From that time on, the going was much slower, but safer, as we wended our way back home with only a bucket or two of blueberries and some grouse to show for a whole month of hunting.

Present day Elliott Highway near Globe Creek

Chapter 3

John Gets Lucky

It was December 15, 1959. The road to Livengood had been officially closed for about three months which meant that the Alaska Highway Department had quit maintaining the Highway. A big sign had been posted about fifteen miles from the start of the road, warning would-be travelers that the road was closed. It said if you continued, you'd be traveling at your own risk.

To further complicate matters, on this specific day the National Weather Service was warning that a storm was imminent. Did any of these warnings deter Stan from continuing with his plans to make the trip? Not on your life! He had the day off, and he was going on this trip, come Hell or High Water. He had talked my Dad into letting him borrow the Jeep, and he was going to Livengood. I really didn't want to see him make that trip by himself, so I invited myself along, and included my little brother Henry in the invitation.

Stan had been visiting with John in Livengood a few months earlier, and learned that one of John's dogs had died. Now, since John had a whole sled-dog team, this didn't seem like such a catastrophe to me, but it apparently did to Stan. So, here we were, in my Dad's little Jeep, heading towards Livengood with a big, wooly dog Stan thought would make a nice early Christmas present for John. And, like the Weather Service had warned, it was starting to snow.

"Don't you think we ought to just wait until spring to deliver this fur ball to John?" I asked.

"No. Do you think we want to live with him all winter?" Stan replied. He did have a good question.

"Why didn't you think of that when you picked him up?" I asked, as the big dog slurped me in the face.

"I didn't know it was going to snow today," he replied, "and it's not often that you can get a purebred retriever for free." I wondered, *who needs a purebred retriever on a dog team?* (I didn't voice the thought out loud, though). Besides, he was really a nice dog. Stan had seen the advertisement for him in the Free Column of the *Fairbanks Daily News Miner*. Stan did have a point about getting such a neat dog for free.

We continued to make our way up the snow-covered road for the approximately fifty miles we had to travel from the sign saying we were traveling at our own risk. The snow began to come down thicker and thicker and the wind began to blow harder and harder. It was a relief to finally reach the top of the hill and see the little town of Livengood lying there snuggly in the valley, with smoke lazily drifting out of its four chimneys.

At that time, Livengood was a thriving community of four permanent, but ancient, residents. The youngest was about seventy-five years old, give or take a few years. The town of Livengood was visited once a week by a mail plane during the winter, weather permitting. But it had been nearly three months since they had seen any vehicular traffic. Most people heeded the sign.

"Wow! We made it," I said as we got out of the Jeep in front of the Livengood

Inn, the establishment owned by John's brother Tony. "Now, don't get to talking too much. We still have to get home, you know."

But, of course, the entire population of the town had heard the motor, and all four had come out to give us their greetings. Nothing would do but that we go into the Livengood Inn. Tony insisted we have a cup of coffee, liberally laced with whisky for Stan and me, . . . and laced with canned milk for my little brother. John and his dog bonded immediately. John decided to call the dog "Lucky," since it was lucky that we'd made it through.

We lingered nearly an hour, and in that time, the wind picked up more, and the snow still came pelting down. There was probably an additional six inches of snow on the road, over and above what it had to begin with, and it was beginning to drift in places.

All fall the daylight had been getting less and less, and now in December, we had fewer than four hours of daylight. We had gotten an early start from home for our venture, but it still had taken us nearly three hours to make the drive. It would take us at least that long to drive back, and there were only about two hours of daylight left. There was no way we could get home before dark, even if we had an uneventful trip like we had on the way up.

After saying our goodbyes, we headed towards home. Some of the snow drifts were getting really hard to get through, and the blowing snow made visibility nearly nonexistent. There were several times when we got stopped in a snowbank, and had to back up and slam into it again and again to get through. But the faithful little Jeep just kept chugging along until …

"What was that?" I asked in a panic. It sounded to me like the Jeep missed a beat.

"We might be getting snow under the hood, and it could be wetting up the engine." Stan calmly replied.

That was not good news. And sure enough, it happened again, and then again.

Suddenly, there was dead silence. The Jeep had died. The heater fan slowly quit whirring when Stan turned off the key, and there was complete silence. Here we were, crossing an arm of Globe Creek, nearly thirty-five miles from civilization, and our transportation had quit on us. "Good Grief," I said, "What do we do now?"

Stan lifted the hood of the Jeep and started trying to figure out what was wrong. He would ask me to try to turn over the engine while he checked for sparks. Then it was, "turn on the lights." "Turn off the key." "Step on the starter," etc.

In the meantime, Henry and I took inventory of our supplies. We had two candy bars, a bag of miniature marshmallows, a thermos of lukewarm coffee, one slightly crushed sandwich, and a can of soda pop. Fortunately, we also had three sleeping bags, winter boots, winter coats, winter hats and gloves, matches, a hatchet, and two flashlights. We could stay warm, even if we were hungry.

Stan climbed back into the Jeep, sat there for a minute in silence, and then finally said, "I think the coil got wet up going through those deep snow banks. There's no spark."

We sat there, as the Jeep began to cool off inside, each of us busy with our own thoughts. Mine ran along the line of *why, oh why, did I ever leave Montana?*

"You know, I think I remember seeing a road grader just over the hill on our way up," Stan said. "It just might have a coil that would work. It's probably not more than half a mile from here. I guess I'll hike up there and see if I'm remembering right. I'll take one of the flashlights, 'cause I know it's going to get dark before I get back." And off he went.

"Henry," I said, "instead of just sitting in this Jeep and getting colder, why don't we build a shelter from the wind and snow and make a fire?"

"Good idea," Henry replied. "I'll get the fire wood."

We trudged out into the blowing snow looking for a good place to build our shelter. We soon found a nice overhang along the creek bank that was almost out of the wind. Henry began collecting any loose piece of wood for a fire he could find, while I collected branches from the spruce trees with our trusty hatchet to put over the shelter and to use as a floor. We worked like beavers for about an hour, and by that time we were ready for a break. Tired, cold, hungry, and wet would be apt descriptions of our condition, but we were in good spirits.

To put it mildly, neither Henry nor I were woodsmen. It took us nearly half of our precious match supply before we had a blaze going. It felt good to relax on a sleeping bag in our snug hide-a-way, and enjoy the warming fire.

"Hey, do you think we could share the sandwich and save the marshmallows for Stan?" Henry asked. I agreed. Food never tasted so good, even a slightly smashed sandwich.

It was beginning to get dark but our fire was roaring, giving us more comfort than heat, as we sat there munching. Then, over the hill came Stan. "Guess what!" he yelled. "I found one; I think it'll work."

It didn't take very long until he had the Jeep running, and we were ready to say goodbye to our nice, cozy shelter. We gathered up our meager pile of remaining supplies, and hauled them back to the Jeep. We gave Stan his dinner, and he said that he'd never tasted such yummy marshmallows.

We were on our way and had gone just a few miles with the blizzard still raging, and the amount of snow steadily increasing, when we came to a place where a spring had caused ice to run across the road during a warm spell. One of the wheels dropped into a hole in the ice with a jolt, and the Jeep sputtered and died again.

"Oh, no!" Henry shouted. "We're too far away from our shelter. Now what?"

"The coil wasn't exactly the right size, and I couldn't find any "duct tape," so I didn't get it mounted very well. I'll bet it fell off with that big bump," Stan said.

Sure enough, he was right. It took just a minute of his work under the hood and we were going again. We were all three very, very happy folks when we saw the back side of that sign that read, "Road Closed, Travel at Your Own Risk!"

Imagine the surprise of the gentleman from the Highway Department when Stan called him the next morning, and told him he had the coil from the road grader that was parked along the Elliott Highway. Mr. DeAngelo graciously allowed us to drop the coil off at his office instead of having to go all the way back to replace it. What a nice guy.

Rose standing by her Dad's Jeep

Chapter 4

High-Centered and No Moose

I was busily tending to my young daughter that day towards the end of August 1960, when telephone rang. Suzie was only a couple of weeks old. While she was a good baby, I still had my hands full, with her and eighteen-month-old Danny. "Can you get that?" I asked Stan … and he did.

He soon came back into the room, and said, "That was your Dad. He wants to go grouse hunting near Livengood tomorrow, and wondered if we'd like to go. Your Mom said she'd watch the kids, if you want to come along. It's only for the day, what do you think?"

Since the next day was Saturday, and Stan's day off, I replied, "I think it would be great fun. And, moose season opened on the twentieth, we can take our rifles in case we see one. If we can get our moose now, you won't have to spend the month of September hunting."

He didn't look pleased about that last statement. He did love his moose hunting trips.

The following day saw us delivering Danny and Sue (and their ton of supplies) to Mom's house, about ten miles from where we lived. Then, Dad, Stan and I crawled into the Jeep, and were off. If you have never ridden in the back seat of one of those old 1941 Willy's Jeeps, you've missed out on a real experience. Not only was it uncomfortable, but if you needed to get out, it took a magician to pry you loose. So, part of the way Stan folded himself down and rode there, so I could have the front seat, and part of the way I rode there.

We were successful in bagging about ten grouse, and were thinking about heading home, when I thought I saw a moose in the brush beside the road. "Stop!" I yelled.

And, the Jeep came to a screeching halt. Dad slowly backed up to about where I thought I'd seen the moose, and we extricated ourselves from the Jeep, with our rifles instead of the shotguns.

Dad said, "You walk that way, and I'll go this way."

Stan took off towards the right, along the roadway berm, and I trailed along behind Dad in the other direction. We were all keeping our eyes peeled on the brush, looking for that moose. It wasn't long before I spotted him, and what a magnificent creature he was. His rack was huge, about the biggest I've ever seen. And, he was just standing there looking back over his shoulder at me. I lined the sights of my gun up on his chest, right behind his front leg, like I'd been taught. Then, I sort of hesitated, waiting for someone else to fire the first shot. There was dead silence.

In my head, I could just hear my Dad saying, "She went off half-cocked, and we didn't get to bring home the meat."

So, I lowered my gun, and looked around for Dad. He was still trudging along the berm, and still looking diligently for the moose. I realized he hadn't seen that sneaky old moose, and Stan was off in the other direction. So, I lined up on the moose again. It was all up to me. Before I could get my sights on him, that big critter just vanished before my very eyes. How can a huge animal with those gigantic horns move so stealthily through the brush? But, he did.

I caught up with Dad, and said, "Why didn't you shoot?"

He replied, "What are you talking about? Shoot at what?"

"That huge moose back there," I said. And, when my Dad went back, he spotted the tracks of this gigantic moose in a mud puddle. But, the moose was long gone. "There's a trail that leads off in the direction the moose went," Dad said. "Let's get Stan, and see if we can't find that moose."

Back in the Jeep we crawled, and went off down a little trail. The farther we went, the thicker the muskeg became, until soon the clumps of muskeg were almost impossible to get over. "I don't want to try to back out," Dad said. "I think there's a clearing just ahead, where we can turn around. We have to give up on the moose."

The Jeep sort of hesitated about that time, and Dad gunned the engine. It leaped forward, and then quit moving altogether, even though the engine was roaring. We all crawled out of the Jeep again, and imagine our surprise to find that the Jeep was perched on top of one of the muskeg humps with all four wheels off the ground.

We were standing there rather stupefied, when there was a huge roar overhead, and a couple of fighter planes buzzed us. I don't think they were higher than thirty-feet above the scraggly trees. How humiliating to be caught with the Jeep perched on that hump! But, perhaps they thought we were just out looking for berries or something, instead of being high-centered.

"Well, this is a fine mess," Dad said. "Any suggestions?"

"I think we can use the jack and jack-up the front wheels, and you can back off," Stan replied. And, that is what we did.

Dad managed to back the Jeep all the way down the trail to the Elliott Highway (even if he hadn't wanted to), and we headed home. Needless to say, the moose was history, no meat in the freezer, and Stan enjoyed his month-long hunting trip. At least we had grouse for dinner.

Our families: l-r: Betty; Dad (Fred); Mom (Dorothy)
holding Sue; Debbie; Henry holding Danny, 1960

Chapter 5

How Did They Do That?

It was the second moose season in November 1960. Stan had just become the proud owner of a 1942 Willy's Jeep. He was so proud of his new acquisition that it was hard to keep the buttons on his shirt from popping off. And, he would no longer have to ask Dad to borrow his Jeep.

One morning, Stan and his good friend Bob, were sitting at our kitchen table, drinking coffee. "I think we should take my Jeep and go hunting." Stan said.

Bob, who loved to hunt, replied: "I thought you'd never ask ... I even brought my rifle, so let's go!" Almost as an afterthought, Bob asked, "Where do you want to go?"

"I think we should go up the Elliott Highway," Stan replied. "Since the road's closed, there shouldn't be much traffic. And I saw some moose sign there a few weeks ago."

The Elliott Highway had been closed, with no maintenance, for over two months.

And a big sign was posted on the road that said, "Road Closed, Travel at Your Own Risk!" After our previous experience of traveling on that road when it was closed, I was quite concerned about this scheme they'd hatched.

"Are you sure you want to go hunting there?" I asked. "What if you get stuck? You can't walk all that way home, and I'm not sure anyone could find you. Remember last year when we took Lucky up for John? We were lucky to get out alive."

"Don't worry," Stan replied. "If Bob and I don't show up for work, the Air Force will send out a search party." Both Stan and Bob worked in the Teletype Maintenance Shop at Ladd Air Force Base. And, there was Stan's, "don't worry" bit again

Even though I was busy worrying, I dutifully packed them a lunch, kissed Stan goodbye (thinking it might be for the last time), and watched as the Jeep disappeared down the road.

I had just settled down with my second cup of coffee, when I heard the kitchen door open and in walked Stan!

"I see you finally got some sense," I said. "Glad you decided not to go hunting on that road."

"I have a surprise for you, old worry-wart." He replied. "Bob and I both have our moose, and I just came back for some rope and chain so we can pull them out to the road, and load them in the Jeep."

"You've got to be kidding," I replied. You haven't been gone more than an hour. How could you already have two moose?" My voice probably was more than a little skeptical. I just knew he was joking with me.

"Well, we were just going up the hill the other side of the spring, even before we got to where they've closed the road," he said, "when we spotted two young bulls right near the road. Bob got one, and I got the other. And, where they are, we can just drag them up on the road to load in the Jeep. Since it was so close to home, I decided to come and get the ropes and stuff, while Bob is cleaning them."

He went into the garage, and reappeared with bundles of rope and other equipment and supplies in his arms, crawled back into the Jeep, and away he went. Sure enough, they showed up several hours later, with two bull moose tied onto the Jeep. It was quite a sight to behold, and we were thankful that the freezer would be full for the long winter ahead.

Rybachek family in 1962: l-r Rose holding Danny and Sue, Stan holding Sallie

Chapter 6

Good Advice

It was a beautiful spring day in March of 1962. The temperature had dropped to minus 20°F the night before, which was kind of cold for that time of year. However, the sun was shining brightly, the temperatures had risen to above freezing by 10:00 a. m. and the snow was beginning to melt. Everything was right with the world, when the telephone rang.

"Hello!" I said.

"Hey, how would you kids like to take a little ride?" It was my Dad on the phone. "You know Curt has gone out camping with his dog team, and I think it would be fun to go see how he's getting along." Curt Reed worked with my Dad on the Air Force base, plowing snow.

"If he went with the dog team, how can we visit him?" I asked. Always seeming to have to point out the obvious, I added, "We don't have a dog team."

"He said he wasn't very far from where the road closed sign is, and I'm sure we can just walk up to his camp from there. And, Mom said she'd babysit."

Any excuse for me to get out of the house. So, Stan and I bundled the kids up in their winter coats, and took them over to Mom's to stay while we were gone. The little darlings loved to visit with Grandma. Not only was she the best cookie cook around, but she let them do things that they never got to do at home. She always said that it was a Grandma's duty to spoil her grandkids.

We were soon on our way in the Jeep. There were five of us: Dad, Stan, two of my siblings (Betty and Henry), and I. We drove up the Elliott Highway, and it seemed like no time at all until we reached the big snow berm on the Highway, where the maintenance crews had stopped maintaining the road. Parking the Jeep in front of that familiar warning sign, we made sure our boots were fastened, and started out along the track. It was easy to walk on the track; the snow had turned to ice where it had been disturbed and, if you didn't fall off the beaten trail, everything was fine.

This year, the roadblock was in the middle of the Willow Creek Flats. It was only about a hundred yards from where there was a bridge that went over Willow Creek. The creek had glaciered quite a bit by this time of year, and ice was over the road in several places. "Be careful," my Dad warned. "Don't fall through. It could be deep; and there probably is water under the ice."

We inched our way across the glacier, and sure enough, you could hear water running under the ice on the trail. "Be careful!" Dad again cautioned us. But, the ice bridge held, and we were soon across the worst looking part of the glacier.

I was really surprised when we rounded a bend in the road and came upon Curt's camp. He had his dogs pegged out on various short runs. He also had a tent pitched. The campfire was burning merrily along with a coffee pot bubbling in its midst and sending up an odor that smelled heavenly. We each pulled up a stump, and enjoyed a delicious cup of coffee. He seemed to be enjoying his camping trip extremely well. We had a good visit.

As we were getting ready to leave, Dad told us once again to be careful. He was really worried that someone might fall through the ice on the way out. We headed down the hill, and across the flat to where the glacier started. It looked like the ice had melted a little bit while we were gone, but the trail still seemed to be solid.

"You kids form a single file, and be careful!" Dad said. "I'll bring up the rear, and make sure everyone makes it across safely."

Everything was going well, and we were almost all on the other side of the creek, when we heard a loud "crack" behind us. Looking back, there stood Dad nearly thigh deep in water. The ice had finally given way, just as he was concerned that it might, and guess who got caught?

Fortunately, it wasn't far to the Jeep, and with the heater roaring all the way home, Dad managed to escape even a hint of frostbite. Even so, he was sure happy to see the lights of home.

Chapter 7

Tragedy at Ben's Cabin

It was an early Saturday morning in July 1962. Stan and my Dad had leased a couple of mining claims on Wilbur Creek from our friend, John. During the summer of 1962, my parents moved their family into the town of Livengood. Livengood was nearly a ghost town, but it still had quite a few livable cabins. John had told my parents that a two-room cabin near his cabin was vacant, and since he as good as owned it, he would be happy if they moved in. So, they did.

Stan was still in the Air Force, but got two to three days a week off. When he worked a double shift, he'd get three days off, and if he just worked his normal shift, he'd get two days. Stan, our three small babies and I traveled to Livengood almost every weekend on his days off, and we stayed with Mom and Dad in the cabin. Mom, with my siblings Betty (thirteen), Henry (nine), and Debbie (seven), would usually stay at the cabin with Danny (forty-three months), Sue (twenty-three months), and Sallie (eleven months). After breakfast, Stan and Dad would usually drive to the mining claims to work. I sometimes stayed with Mom and the kids but often I would go with the guys.

On this sunny day, there was a job that the guys figured needed more than their four hands to complete, so they'd asked me along. Stan, Dad and I got into Dad's Jeep, and away we went. As we left the cabin in Livengood, I said, "Stan, what do you think about that bear last night?"

"He's getting too friendly." Stan replied. "Imagine him peeking through the window like that. No wonder your Mom nearly had a heart attack."

Mom had gotten up in the middle of the night to get a drink of water. She dipped into the water bucket with the old tin dipper, and was taking a big swallow from the dipper, when she glanced up towards the window right behind the water pail. There stood a black bear, with both of his front feet on the window, and his nose pressed to the glass, peering in. She screamed and flung the dipper on the floor, racing out of the room and spewing water towards the window. By the time Dad and Stan got out of their beds and grabbed their rifles, the bear was long gone. He was probably just as scared as Mom.

"Do you think he might bother the babies?" I asked.

"Probably not, but we'd better not let them out by themselves. Old John set some snares for the bugger, and I'll bet we won't have to worry for long."

In 1962, the road into and out of Livengood wended its way up a steep hill for about a mile, and had several steep switchbacks. Just before you got to the top of the hill, there was a switchback where you could look down on a picturesque cabin. The cabin belonged to Ben Falls and his wife. Ben mined on Wilbur Creek, the same creek where we had our claims. When we rounded the switchback, we noticed that there was a lot of smoke coming out of the chimney of Ben's cabin.

"Boy, Old Ben must really have a fire going," I said. "I wonder what he's burning."

"I have no idea," Stan replied. "But whatever it is, it sure is putting out a lot of smoke."

We continued on our way; after fording the river, we were pretty surprised to see Ben in the distance, hard at work on his claims. Ben had a small, tarpaper shack on his claim that he sometimes stayed in overnight, when he didn't feel like driving the nearly ten miles to his cabin. However, he usually went home at night, because his wife was quite crippled by arthritis and was not very mobile. Ben did most of the cooking and cleaning for her.

We didn't think much more about it since our minds were on our task and that bear. We completed the task, ate our lunch, and then headed back to the cabin. As we were going down the hill into Livengood, we saw that Ben's cabin was gone, and only a black spot remained. Once we arrived back in Livengood, we learned that Ben's cabin had burned to the ground that morning, and his wife had died in the fire. The consensus was that she had a chimney fire. We wished we had thought to go check on her.

Several nights later, the nosy bear did find its way into one of John's snares, and we didn't have to worry about that bear any longer.

Chapter 8

Down is Sometimes Better Than Up

What had I gotten myself into? Here I was, a lady of twenty-four years (and feeling ever one of those twenty-four years), who hadn't been on a bike for at least ten of those years, out trying to keep up with some young sprouts on a bike. It all happened like this.

On this weekend in early July, Stan, I and our three kids, had driven to Livengood to continue our work of developing the mining claims. There wasn't much room in the cabin my folks were staying in, so we'd made our beds on the floor. After breakfast, Stan and Dad had driven over to the mine to work. On this Saturday, I had not gone with them.

My siblings had been after me for several weeks to join them in riding bikes over to the mining claims. Their plan was that we'd catch a ride home with Dad and Stan. I had finally agreed, and here I was.

The hill coming out of Livengood was steep, so we talked Mom into driving us to the top of the hill in Stan's Jeep, and hauling the bikes for us. That left only about nine miles of road to the mine, but I figured that most of it was downhill after all, when you drove in the car, it seemed that way. Boy was I wrong. I had forgotten that the mining claims were *upstream* from Livengood, which, if I'd thought about it, was not a good indicator that we would be going mostly downhill to get there.

We had the dickens of a time trying to get all the bikes and our supplies loaded into the Jeep. We had to tie the bikes on top, and neither Mom nor I was an expert knot-tier. Then, we had to find room for all of us, including the three little ones, in that tiny Jeep. After a massive struggle, we finally got everything loaded (including us), and made it to the "top" of the hill. My siblings and I got onto our bikes and waved a cheerful goodbye to Mom and the babies.

This was before the advent of those fancy ten-speed bikes that you see people cruising up and down hills on today. I did have a twenty-four-inch bike, but my younger sister, Debbie, was peddling away on a sixteen-inch bike. Let me tell you, it took lots of turns of the wheel for her to keep up.

It was a beautiful summer day. The sun was shining brightly, not a cloud in the sky (except for a cloud of mosquitoes that thought we were fair game). It was pretty easy going for the first mile or so, because it *was* mostly downhill. We just had to be sure we didn't get up too big of a head of steam. Gravel roads are notorious for surprises.

We stopped about every half-mile to renew our mosquito repellant. Even being soaked to the hilt with repellant, the mosquitoes were ferocious. I had forgotten to bring my sunglasses, and had to stop several times to dig one of the little critters out of my eyes. That smarted!

We had traveled about three miles, when we finally decided it was time to stop for a snack. Stretching out in the shade of a nice tree, we ate one of our sandwiches, swigged down some of our water, and had a nice rest. It was fun to wave at the lone car that went by. There wasn't much traffic on the road that particular Saturday. The thought had crossed my mind that we could hitch a ride, if someone we knew came by with a pickup. But, the kids were happy to finally be riding their bikes, and raring to go.

Back on the road again, we were slowly walking our bikes up a hill, when a black bear came out along the edge of the trees near the road. It just stood there, staring at us. I suppose it wondered what kind of critters we were, with our wheels rolling slowly along. We just ignored him, and soon he disappeared back into the brush where he came from. We were happy about that.

We had just topped the hill, when a little cloud came and hid the sun. Looking up, we noticed that it was a little black cloud, and just like the song, it sat right down and cried … right over us. We quickly donned our windbreakers, and were pretty happy when the cloud moved on and let the sun shine again. We were a bit damp, but not completely soaked. However, the rain had wreaked havoc with our mosquito repellant, and the mosquitoes had a field day until we got more repellant on. Good thing we had brought along a plentiful supply.

At about the seven-mile mark, we decided to stop at a nearby spring. By that time, our water bottles were nearly empty, and I figured it was time for a long rest. It was difficult trying to find the spring to fill our bottles, which surprised me. The water was running down the ditch, like it always had. But, the spring itself was buried in a lot of mud that had recently washed into the rock bowl somebody had built many years before. We had to scoop out the mud, and wait for nearly half an hour for the mud to settle out of the water before we could fill our bottles. Of course, the wait was wonderful for this old lady. I still wasn't ready to leave when the water had cleared, and we had our jugs refilled. Who agreed to this bike ride anyway? But, the kids were ready to go, so soon we were on the road again.

By the time we came to the juncture where our access road turned off the Highway, we were all getting pretty darned tired. All of us were happy to know that the end was in sight. It was only about a mile from the turn-off to where we ought to find Dad's Jeep, if all went well. But, going across the flat presented several problems to a bicycle rider. Most of the road was under water. Not deep water, but mud holes full of water. If we were very careful, we could manage to stay in the tall grass in the middle of the road, and try to keep our feet dry. Rubber boots would have been nice, but of course, we were pedaling in sneakers instead of rubber boots.

Road across the flat, difficult to navigate on a bike

We, and our cloud of mosquitoes, finally arrived at the river. We hadn't thought about how to get across that, either. After a discussion with my siblings, I decided I'd take my shoes off, wade across the river and push the bike. That way, I'd have nice dry shoes when I got to the other side. Both Betty and Debbie decided that was the way they would do it, too, but Henry had other ideas. He decided he could ride across the river, if he got a good run for it.

While Betty, Debbie, and I sat down near the riverbank, removing our shoes, Henry backed-up and got his run. He was really going fast when he hit the water. Water spewed up like a tremendous waterspout from his tires, and his tireless, churning legs pumped for all he was worth—but it wasn't enough. He had only gotten about a quarter of the way across, when he started slowing down, and before he knew what was happening, the bike came to a halt, and nearly fell over. He did manage to catch himself with a tremendous splash, but he was wet clear up to his waist.

The rest of us walked, pushing our bikes through the river. We stopped on the other side to put on our dry socks and shoes, and perhaps we may have teased a drenched Henry just a little bit, as we pointed out how nice our dry socks felt. He did look like a drowned rat.

Fortunately, the sun had come out again, and it wasn't long before he was dry, except for his shoes. They took quite a long time to dry.

It was a relief to find the Jeep right where we thought it would be, and park our bikes. The old one of the bunch was completely exhausted, but the young ones were raring to try it again. We never did.

I learned a valuable lesson on that jaunt, which I was in no wise willing to repeat!

Livengood Post Office

Chapter 9

Bear Necessities

Stan had been looking forward to moose season for many months, and scheming as to how he'd be able to go just about anywhere with his new-to-him weapons carrier. He had been the successful bidder at the Army Salvage yard on a 1953 Dodge three-quarter ton Military Weapons Carrier that we'd dubbed the Weps. He was all set to see just where he could go with it; and hopefully bag a moose at the same time. He had taken leave for the whole month of September, so he could really enjoy himself.

"Are you planning on taking the trailer, and cutting wood for John and Tony again?" I asked.

"Yep, and if your Mom will watch the kids, you can come with me," he said. "We'll hunt in the morning and evening, and haul wood during the day. And, maybe we can pick some berries while we're at it. With the Weps, we can haul a lot more wood than we could with the Jeep and trailer." This sounded exciting to me, since I loved to be in the great outdoors.

The first day of Stan's leave, September 1, 1962 rolled around. He and I took the kids to Grandma's house, packed up our supplies, and headed up the Elliott Highway. Mom and Dad had moved back to Fairbanks from their little cabin in Livengood, for school. Stan and I decided we'd rather camp in a tent than live in the cabin they'd vacated. So, we set up camp near the West Fork of the Tolovana River near Livengood. This was a familiar stomping ground, since Stan had been hunting in that area for several years, and I'd even joined him once upon a time.

Bright and early the next morning, we were out checking our favorite spots for moose ... none in the First Lake ... none in the Second Lake ... nor was there any in the Third Lake. We wondered if those moose had a calendar marked, "Make Yourself Scarce during Moose Season!"

Scarce the moose continued to be. We diligently hunted morning and evening, and cut and hauled wood during the day. And, as the days blended one into another, I became less and less enthusiastic about our "hunting trip." Besides, I missed the kids.

One morning a couple of weeks into our trip, Stan said to me, "Come on, sleepyhead, and get out of the sack."

"Do I have to?" I replied. I was all snug and warm in my sleeping bag, and I knew that it was downright cold outside the tent. Every morning it was the same thing. Stan wanted to be up and about way before daylight, while I thought that staying in the sleeping bag would be a better option. After all, we had been up early road hunting for nearly fourteen days, and still hadn't found anything to shoot at, except bunnies and grouse.

"If you don't get up, I'll just throw you into the Weps, sleeping bag and all," he told me, with a wicked grin.

"You know, that doesn't sound like such a bad idea. That is, if I have to go with you. I could just stay here this morning," was my reply. "But, if I do need to come with you, get me a cup of coffee, will you?"

I was quite surprised when I felt myself being lifted bodily in his arms, and hoisted into the navigator's seat of the

Weps. I really thought he was bluffing. However, it wasn't long before I had a nice, hot cup of coffee, so I couldn't be too angry. We were soon on the move, and just in time, too, because daylight was just dawning.

We had been very successful in getting small game. We mainly had lived on fried grouse and rabbit for the past two weeks, and found them to be delicious. But so far, no other game had shown itself.

We drove towards Manley Hot Springs, stopping at every vantage point to check whether any wayward moose was having breakfast in lakes, along gravel pits, or anywhere the brush allowed visibility. It was another beautiful day, after the sun had risen, and it warmed up. The temperature had dipped to about 30°F during the night, but with the warm sunshine, it wasn't long before I could shed my sleeping bag, and get serious about our hunting.

We had just come out of a timbered area into a large flat covered with blueberry bushes and brush, when we saw a nice sized black bear making his way along the hillside across a ravine. He was quite a distance from us, and seemed very unconcerned about our presence. He was devouring blueberries as rapidly as he could stuff them in his mouth.

"Do you think we ought to try for him?" I asked.

"I don't see why not, we don't have anything else to show for all our hunting." Stan replied, as he swung the Weps over to the shoulder of the road and parked.

We got out, loaded shells into our guns, and began to stalk the bear. He was still unconcerned about us, as he continued to have breakfast. When we figured we were within shooting range, we settled in, rested our guns on our knees, and started shooting.

It sounded like the Fourth of July for a while. But, the bear just continued to amble along, eating blueberries. We continued shooting, and he continued eating.

Finally, he fell. "I think we got him!" I yelled. "Let's go see."

"Be careful," Stan cautioned. "He might just be wounded, and a wounded bear is nothing to fool around with." We approached our bear with caution, but he didn't move. He was ours.

As we started the skinning process, we were quite surprised to find fourteen bullet holes in his hide, and almost all of them were in the rib cage where we had aimed. He was one tough old bear. Thanks to him, we didn't have to go home empty handed. That bear was the only big game we bagged on that trip. Bear meat makes delightful sausage. And, the hide makes a beautiful rug. So, we were not disappointed with our trophy.

Bear

Chapter 10

Pie Wood is Not as Easy as Pie

Stan and I were still hunting and hauling wood that September of 1962, enjoying our delightful camp on the banks of the West Fork of the Tolovana River. During the middle of each day, we cut wood and hauled it into Livengood for John and Tony. We felt like we were doing a good deed and helping them out. Having participated in the gold rush in about 1914, they were both getting along in years. We enjoyed visiting with them, and they had some interesting tales to tell.

Besides, when we delivered a load of wood, Tony always set up a free beer or two on his counter. He was the owner and proprietor of the Livengood Inn, which was the only place to get gas or booze for miles around. Stan had hauled him many barrels of gasoline, and many cases of beer, at no charge for the transportation. Tony would sell to anyone that needed gas or liquid refreshments. If he liked you, the price for a gallon of gas might be $1.50, but if he didn't know you, you could expect to pay upwards of $5.00 a gallon. He had a habit of selling the beer at the same inflated prices—it seemed like the more a person drank, the higher he charged for a bottle of beer. Was he a character? You bet. But, he liked us, because we always were pushovers for anything he wanted.

One September day, we had been out hunting early in the morning, and as usual, had seen neither hide nor hair of any moose. Back to our camp we went, where we enjoyed our breakfast of pancakes. We got the trailer hitched up for another load of wood. We had spotted a great stand of what John called "pie wood" when we were out that morning, and figured it would be a good plan to go back and harvest that. "Pie wood" was John's name for standing trees from an area that had burned several years before. The standing trees burned enough to have died, but had not burned completely. They were left standing, bleached white by time, and really made a hot fire when burned in the stove. Those trees were great for baking pies; thus, their moniker.

We made our way back to the stand of pie wood, and it was every bit as good as we had figured. "I think we can just knock over the entire tree, and load it on the trailer," Stan said. "That way, we won't have to use the chainsaw on this hard-wood."

His plan was that *he* would knock them over, and pull the roots loose from the moss, and *I* would drag them to the trailer. Then, when I had a fairly large stack by the trailer, he'd give up knocking them over, and we'd load them in the trailer. We worked hard for several hours, and by that time, we had a huge load on the trailer. The trailer wasn't very long, but some of the trees were. Stan tied them down quite securely, so they would stay on the trailer, but still some of the trees had about two-thirds still hanging off the back end of the trailer. Sometimes they would even drag on the ground; since it was a gravel road all the way into Livengood, we figured once we got to the road, it wouldn't hurt anything if they did drag once in a while.

This was one heavy load of wood. We had to use four-wheel drive to get it moving down the little trail we were on. I was very relieved when we finally arrived at the Elliott Highway. If we continued to go at the snail's pace we had been traveling, it would take us two days to get back to the town of Livengood. Now that we were on the Highway again, the going was much faster.

The brakes on the Weps were not as trust-worthy as brakes are today, and of course, there were no brakes on the trailer. But, we went slow and easy. We were coming down the final hill into the West Fork of the Tolovana River, when the brakes heated up on the Weps, and just quit braking. Stan had the Weps in low gear, but even that started to chatter, and we began going faster and faster down the hill. Not only were we picking up speed, but the load was very heavy, and it became more and more difficult to steer the Weps. We started wobbling back and forth on the road, first little wobbles, then bigger and bigger ... and faster and faster we went.

"What's happening?" I yelled in fear.

"I can't steer!" Stan replied in a panic. "The load on the trailer must be picking up the front wheels of the Weps, and I can barely keep it on the road."

By this time, we were nearly taking the whole width of the road on our swings, and I was looking at the depth of the ditches, figuring that the very next swing would put us into one or the other. Suddenly, there was a loud "Bang," and we quit swinging, and then started slowing down.

"What happened?" I asked.

"Whew," Stan replied, "I think we lost our load." And sure enough, there was our pie wood, scattered all over the Highway and the ditch.

"Boy, if my rope hadn't broken when it did, I think we would have turned over." Stan said with relief. "I'm glad I didn't tie those trees on any better."

We decided that it would be smart to make two trips to haul the pie wood the rest of the way into Livengood, and we also figured it would be wise if we cut the long ones in half. We loaded up the trees that were in the road, and hauled them into Livengood. The ones in the ditch could be hauled the next day, since we had hunting to do.

We continued for another week, hauling wood to Livengood during the middle hours of the day. Sometimes we cut down dead trees, and cut them into blocks. Other times, we were lucky to find a supply of pie wood. We figured we had at least a five-year supply for both old timers. We were really surprised the next year to discover that they were out of wood. How could they burn all that wood? The answer to that question was quite a while in coming.

We decided to leave our idyllic camping spot by the river, and go home early. We had one bear hide and several grouse to show for our month-long hunting trip.

Sallie with Red Dog and his mother, Lady.

Chapter 11

This Dog Will Hunt

Ever since Stan and I had been married, we had at least one dog for company. Our first had been a cocker spaniel/terrier mix that traveled the Alcan Highway with us. Soon after we moved to the North Pole area, he picked up some poison and met his demise.

After we lost him, our good friend Bob brought us a very expensive Labrador retriever. This dog, True Blue Jackson III, had some outstanding blood lines. He had been bred to be a show dog, but he was very timid. When taken to a retriever show, he cowered down because of all the noise and people, and would not retrieve. In a fit of rage, his owner threatened to shoot him. Bob brought him to us. The only condition was that we not show him. He was a highly trained retriever, and he and Stan enjoyed many hunting trips for grouse and ducks. We called him "True," or "Troop" and he was a great companion for many years.

I really enjoyed the Lab, but, I had always wanted a beagle. One day we saw an ad in the paper for a female beagle, and were able to snag her. Soon she had a litter of six puppies. Most of them were the normal tri-color of a beagle, but one was different. He had a big streak of white going across his back. Danny was just two years old when the puppies were born, and was just learning to talk. He said, "Look at that red one." From that time on, his name was Red Dog; we had Red Dog for years.

One day in the spring of 1963, we made a trip to our mining property. We were working on a cabin that John had given us permission to repair and live in. We intended to live in that cabin for the upcoming winter. It was a nice log cabin, but was leaning badly, and we were afraid that a good breeze might blow it into the ravine. We jacked it up to straighten it, and nailed some two-by-fours on to keep it straight. The cabin also had a floor problem, and many boards needed to be replaced. It was a busy weekend, and we were all tired and cranky. We crowded into the Weps (dogs and all) and headed down the Elliott Highway towards North Pole.

Red Dog had a history of getting car sick. When he started getting sick, he would drool and lick his lips. It was prudent to pull over to the side of the road and let him out so he could breathe the nice fresh air and get rejuvenated. For some reason, he had more trouble with car sickness on this trip. We were forced to made several stops for him before we reached the hill descending to the Willow Creek Bridge. On that hill, he started drooling and licking again.

"We better stop and let Red Dog out again," I said. Stan grumbled a bit, but soon pulled the Weps over to the side of the road and we let the dog out. He seemed happy to get out, and was breathing deeply. Suddenly, he spotted a rabbit. Being a beagle, he could not resist that temptation. Like a flash, he forgot his sickness, and went nosily after the rabbit.

"What do we do now?" I asked, "do you think he'll come back soon? What if he runs into a wolf or a lynx? He'll be their dinner!" He was making a lot of noise, which was echoed off the hills.

"I guess we'll have to just wait and hope he shows up," Stan replied. "I reckon he'd scare any wolf or lynx, with all that noise. Don't you have some snacks?"

Yes, I did, so we had our sandwiches and drank some water. Before long, the kids were getting tired of waiting, and so were we. We could hear Red Dog baying as he followed his bunny, first on one side of the highway, then the other. Sometimes he would be near, and sometimes we could barely hear him.

"For two cents, I'd just go and leave him," Stan said. "I don't think he'll ever give up and come back."

"We better give him a bit more time," I said. "It would be a shame to leave him."

Sure enough, about two hours later, he did return … panting and looking happy. It was a relief to scold him and load him back in the truck. He managed to get all the way home without slobbering and slurping again. We arrived home tired, crankier, and much later than we intended. Stan just had time to get a little rest before he had to get ready for work the next day.

Needless to say, on the next trip with Red Dog, we took a rope along, so if he needed air, he could get outside, but would not be able to go on another hunting trip.

Chapter 12

Planting a Tree in the Flat

It was the second day of moose season that August of 1963. We had been living in our cabin for about three months, and had really been enjoying ourselves. It seemed like there was never a dull moment, and always something to keep us interested. This day was not any different.

The Cabin at the Mining Claims

"I think we should go into Fairbanks today," Stan said, as he got up that early morning, and began building a fire in the kitchen stove. "I need some supplies for my trap line, and this looks like a good, rainy day to go. Besides, since it's raining, there's not much I can do outside."

"Okay," I said. "I'll get breakfast ready, and get the kids dressed, and we can leave in an hour or so."

Breakfast was a hurried affair, and I quickly packed some sandwiches for the trip. The kids were always hungry, and Stan and I could usually eat something, too. In just under an hour, we were all loaded in the Weps, and headed across the river. We were lucky that the river hadn't risen during the night, and we could still cross it. It was just drizzling lightly, as we headed into the flat. We were happy that the pounding rain had ceased.

The access road into the cabin led across a flat area of boggy tundra. In the 1930s, the old timers had chopped down trees, and laid them side-by-side in a corduroy pattern across the boggy tundra; then covered them with a thin layer of gravel, and this was our access road.

Often, one of the trees would rise out of the gravel on the road, and we would have to remove it. We had placed many loads of gravel on the road to stabilize it ever since we first started developing the mine. Since it traversed across the tundra, it was treacherous if you missed the track.

We were making our way down the access road when Stan said, "Look over there. That's where I spotted a moose just a couple of days ago just before the start of moose season, and he had a big rack."

As he said this, he pointed towards a stand of birch trees, and his attention wandered for just an instant. That was enough for the Weps to fall off the gravel on the road, and both wheels on that side went out of sight in the tundra, with water welling up around them. The frame of the Weps was all that was holding us upright, where it rested on the gravel roadbed.

"Wow!" Stan exclaimed. "There's no way, even with four-wheel drive, that the Weps can get out of this mess on its own. I *could* go back and get the dozer, but I hate driving it across the river this time of the year … everything would get wet, and the idlers might freeze and break this winter."

"Well," I said, "there isn't anything for the winch to hook onto either. We have to do something."

"You know," Stan said, "I think I could bury a tree under the moss on the flat. It's thawed out about as much as it ever thaws, and that just might work."

He set off with his trusty axe, and soon came back dragging a fairly large tree. In the meantime, I tried to start digging a hole. What an impossible task. There was no dirt, just moss. Have you ever tried to shovel moss? It was easier when Stan returned with the axe, and he could chop the moss loose. We were disappointed to find that under the approximately three feet of thawed moss, the ground was still frozen solid. You'd think that having sunshine all summer would have thawed the ground, but apparently moss is a very good insulator.

Stan finally got a hole big enough to get his tree buried. Then, he wrapped the winch cable around it, and covered it with the moss he'd removed. But it wasn't substantial enough to even begin to pull the Weps out of its watery hole.

"Go stand on that tree," Stan said to me. "I think with your added weight, it just might be enough to pull us out." Was he insinuating that I was heavy? No, couldn't be.

So, off I went. It was rather scary trying to maintain my balance, as the winch cable tightened, and I tried to stand as heavy as I could. I was very relieved when the Weps actually moved forward a couple of inches ... then a few more, and a few more, and soon it was back on the road where it had started from.

To this day, that tree is still buried in the flat. Sometime many years in the future, someone may wonder what a spruce tree is doing in that spot. But, for that day, we were thankful that it held firm enough for us to get out of our predicament.

We made our way to the Elliott Highway, and were happy to once again have dodged a bullet, as they say. Our trip to town was uneventful. We enjoyed seeing the golden leaves on the birch trees, and even spotted a moose standing in the tundra near the Tolovana River. We got the shopping done, stopped by the Dairy Queen for a delightful ice cream cone, and were soon on our way back to the cabin. We were happy to arrive back home, safe and sound, even if it was after dark.

Moose behind beaver pond near Tolovana River

Chapter 13

Free Enterprise

As I mentioned, my Dad had frosted his lungs in the winter of 1962 by cranking on a bulldozer to get it started in minus 40°F temperatures. Because of this, Dad, Mom and my siblings had pulled up stakes and moved back to Montana. Stan received his discharge from the Air Force in early June of 1963, and since my parents were planning on moving back to the "Lower Forty-Eight," we figured it was an ideal time to move to the mine.

Winter came, and found us snug in our cabin. We had spent quite a bit of time cutting and stockpiling a huge wood pile, and felt like we were ready to face whatever came. But, once again, we were concerned about our friends, John and Tony. Livengood was about ten miles down the Elliott Highway from us. During the winter months, we probably would not be able to visit except by driving a snow machine (what some people call a "snow mobile") or our tracked vehicle, the weasel. Yes, Stan had added to his fleet of surplus military vehicles with the addition of a tracked vehicle. It resembled an open tank with tracks, but was supposed to be amphibious, and we knew it was good for traversing tundra.

"I think I'll stay with John and Tony for a few days, and get them a supply of wood for the winter. They sure seem to go through an awful lot of it," Stan said to me one day in October. "I should go while I can still drive the Weps on the road."

"This would be a good time to go," I replied. "Everything is fine here. And, you can bring back the mail." The mail plane landed in Livengood once a week, weather permitting.

Bright and early the next morning, Stan gathered up his chainsaw and his axe, sleeping bag and other supplies, and was on his way. Since this was the latter part of October, the days were not nearly as long as they had been earlier in the summer. In fact, we found out that down in the valley where the cabin was located, the sun didn't shine at all for about two months during the winter.

A few nights after Stan left, I noticed that the moon was shining brightly on the freshly fallen snow. The kids were in bed sound asleep, so I decided it would be an ideal time to make a quick run to the dump and dump the garbage that had been accumulating all day. I grabbed the garbage can, and slowly made my way along the path, enjoying the beautiful full moon, the shining stars, and the crackling Northern Lights. I was just getting ready to spill the garbage can into the dump when I heard a wolf howl … and it sounded like it was right beside me. I slung that garbage can for all I was worth, and raced back to the safety of the cabin. All that night, I could hear wolves howling—what an eerie sound. Not much rest that night; I kept hoping they would not try to break in!

The next morning, I was very excited and relieved to hear the Weps making its way up the hill. I *had* thought about venturing out to the dump in the daylight, and retrieving the garbage can, but hadn't quite gotten enough courage to do it. I was elated that Stan was back. He had gotten the wood piles restocked for both John and Tony, and brought our mail.

"Guess what I saw in the flat?" he asked. To my blank look, he said, "I found where a whole pack of wolves brought down a moose. There was blood and tracks everywhere."

He hadn't disturbed the scene of the kill, thinking he could set some snares (which he did, but apparently those wolves had gorged themselves, because they never returned to their kill). Their hunt was what accounted for all the wolf howls that kept me awake the night before. It was mighty comforting having him back home again.

The very next time we went into Livengood to get our mail, we were surprised to see that Tony had put up a sign. It read, "WOOD FOR SALE." No wonder he and John had been going through so much wood all those years. The old shysters had been selling the wood that Stan had been cutting for them. Talk about Free Enterprise … it was free on our end, and enterprise on theirs! Needless to say, Stan never went cutting wood for them again.

Chapter 14

Driving on Thin Ice

"We can go to town tomorrow!" Stan hollered, as he bounded through the door. "Our check finally came. Get ready." He had just returned from checking the mail in Livengood that late October day in 1963.

We had been looking for that check for nearly a month. Due to a cash flow problem, we had not been able to fully lay in the stock of food stuffs we thought we would need to see us through the winter. We were concerned because the first snow had come, and the Elliott Highway between Livengood and Fairbanks had been officially closed to traffic for about six weeks.

While there had been some chilly weather after the closure, not very much snow had fallen. We were having a warm spell, with the temperatures hovering around the 20-30°F range, but snow was expected. If we were to get provisions, now was our chance. With our four-wheel drive weapons carrier, we should have no trouble making the 70+ miles into Fairbanks. "So, what's the plan?" I asked Stan.

"I think we better plan on spending the night in Fairbanks, 'cause we don't want to be traveling when it's dark if we can help it. So, I think we ought to get up early, leave right before daybreak, and hope we don't have any trouble along the way," he replied

"What about the dogs?" I asked. We still had a beagle and a Labrador.

"They should be okay in the house while we're gone. I know it's a long time for them, but if we leave them plenty of food and water, and put down some newspapers for them to use if they have to, they should be okay." Stan replied.

Sunday morning found us scurrying around, getting the kids organized with overnight clothes; finding lots of warm blankets and sleeping bags for the ride; packing a lunch and drinks; getting the dogs all settled in for their prolonged stay home alone; stoking the two stoves with slow burning logs and getting the Weps gassed and ready to go.

As we all clambered into the Weps about 9:30 a.m., I suddenly wondered, *had I shut off the gas fire under the coffee pot?* ... so back to the house; unlock the door; and check the fire on the gas stove. Of course, it was not burning.

The trip was beautiful. There was about a foot of snow in most places, with large flakes floating gently to the ground. The only tracks on the Highway were those of rabbit, moose, fox, lynx and an occasional wolf. No tracks left by any human. The kids and I played a game trying to be the first to spot a new track, and identify it. We only took time out from our game to admire the beauty of the trees in their winter clothes.

We had traveled about half way to Fairbanks, when we came to a patch of very thick ice that went completely across the road. This was where a spring ran in the summertime. We had often stopped there during the summer to get a cold drink of fresh water. Apparently, it had continued running after freeze-up, and had created a large ice field. Stan walked out on the ice, and decided that there were no hidden crevasses to fall in, so we eased our way across the flow. It was our first experience at finding a glacier on the road. Unfortunately, it would not be our last!

Just a short distance around the hill, we came to another glacier. This one, too, was fairly smooth, but also quite a hefty field of ice. Stan again checked for any crevasses, and finding none, we proceeded on our way.

It was so beautiful as we neared the crest of Wickersham Dome. Large flakes of snow were drifting down from the sky. There had been a lot of wind during the recent months, and it had sculpted some interesting drifts. Well, interesting that is, until we found one on the road that was anything but sociable. "I think I'd better chain-up all four wheels for this one," Stan said, as we came to that particularly long and deep drift. While he was doing that, the kids and I walked around looking at the numerous tracks of wild animals and throwing snowballs at each other.

With chains, we had no trouble breaking through the drift and topping the hill. "It's all downhill from here." Stan said.

As we came down the hill to the first little creek, we suddenly spotted a huge ice field, and this one was completely across the road. It was about four feet deep as it reached the road, but then it sloped off towards the canyon as it crossed the road. We just stopped and stared at this roadblock.

"I might be able to take the axe, and cut a trench for our lower wheel to sit in, and it probably wouldn't come out of the trench. We could probably get across." Stan said with quite a bit of uncertainty in his voice.

"*Probably?*" I echoed. "I don't like the sound of that. Cutting a trench for the lower wheels would make the Weps tipsier than it would be if you just drove across, and being so tipsy, it could easily slide right off the road. Then, where would we be? That looks like a fairly steep drop-off on the downhill side."

"Well, if I did make the trench, and the lower wheels slid out of it, there's always a chance the upper wheels would catch in it and stop the slide," he said, with just a little stronger hint of confidence.

"What if you took the axe and carved a trench for the upper wheels to go in?" I asked. "That way, it would sort of level out the Weps, and maybe cut down the chances for a slide."

"Do we really need to go to town?" Stan asked, more to himself than me. "Actually, I guess we'd better go forward, 'cause there's no place to turn around, and I don't think I could back up that hill. So, I guess we have to go on."

I was surprised when Stan took my suggestion about the trench for the upper wheels, and got busy chopping with his axe. The kids and I followed along behind and cleaned the ice pieces out of the trench. It took about forty minutes to get the trench completed.

"You and the kids stay here, and I'll drive the Weps over." Stan said. "Then, once I'm on the other side, you can walk over."

He gingerly eased the Weps into the trench with his upper wheels. As I had predicted, this left it only slightly tipped. Slowly and carefully he made his way across the glacier, and we all heaved a collective sigh of relief when he was safely across.

We gingerly made our way over the ice, and crawled back into the Weps.

We continued along our way, until we topped the next ridge and started down. Low and behold, there was another glacier, of about the same size and shape as the previous one. "Well, we know what to do with this one." Stan said as he jumped out of the Weps. He grabbed his axe, and in about thirty minutes with the full crew working together, we were back on the road, again.

Over the next hill, guess what? We ran into the Granddaddy of all glaciers. It must have been eight feet high, thirty feet wide, and sloped off just like the other two were. "Wow! What do we do about that?" I asked.

"We have to go through it," Stan replied. "We can't possibly go back over those other two, since I can't turn around, and there's no way to back up through them." Grabbing his axe, he began to make the trench.

The kids and I crawled out of the Weps, got our damp gloves on our hands, and began to clear the trench of ice splinters. Trenching and clearing was a lengthy process, since the glacier was so big. It took a good hour and a half to get the trench dug on this one. The sun had been gone for some time, and it was starting to get really dark. We used the headlights from the Weps to finish the last of the trench. However, with the lazily drifting snowflakes, it was awesomely beautiful, even with the nagging thought, *just how many more of these glaciers are we going to find before we get to the maintained road?*

Stan eased the Weps into the big trench, and made his way across the glacier without a hitch. We all heaved another collective sigh of relief. As the kids and I made our way across the glacier, Sue slipped, and away she went—right over the edge of the glacier. She was easy to find, though, because of the high volume of noise she was making. She was scared, but wasn't hurt, and while it took a bit of time for us to get her safely back on the glacier without all of us joining her, we finally succeeded.

Around the bend we drove, and at the next bend in the road, there was another glacier. This one was only about a foot deep, and flat on top. How wonderful! As we made our way down the hills toward Fairbanks, we found several more baby glaciers, but none that needed a trench. We were all happy when we finally found the plowed road, and could read the back of the sign that said, "Road Closed, Travel at Your Own Risk!"

Our friends were surprised to see us and we had a good visit. Then, the next morning, we loaded up the Weps with enough staples to see us through the winter. "Do you think our trenches will be frozen shut?" I asked.

"I don't think so, since it snowed most of the night, and was fairly warm" Stan replied. "We might have trouble seeing our tracks and trying to stay in them, though, because of the new snow. But, I think we'll be okay. I have an idea, though. I think we ought to take some ashes along for traction."

That's what we did. A five-gallon bucket of warm ashes sat by my feet near the heater. When we reached the first trenched glacier, Stan took a coffee can and spread ashes where our lower wheels would go. The trench was still open, although it had filled with water. The water hadn't frozen solid yet; just a skim of ice on top that the wheels easily broke through.

We reached home in only four hours, where it had taken us seven and a half to get to town the previous day. The two dogs were very happy to see us. They had done an excellent job of guarding the house. Some of the logs were still smoldering in the barrel stove; the house was warm; and the dogs hadn't even had an accident all the time we were gone. They were happy to get outside though, and we were happy to be home with our winter food supply. The dogs deserved their treat, and we deserved a rest.

Troop is a reluctant sled dog for Sue, Sallie and Danny

Chapter 15

Trouble with Santa's Sleigh

What a problem we had! We had ordered Christmas presents for the kids from Sears and Roebuck. Unfortunately, the weather had turned nasty, and the mail plane (which usually came in every Friday to the town of Livengood) hadn't been able to land for three weeks due to inclement weather. Here it was, just five days before Christmas, and there wasn't a present in the house. The kids had been excitedly talking about what Santa would bring them. However, without a miracle, Santa would be empty-handed. Probably the kids wouldn't be excited about a boiled egg in their stockings, but that was one of the options I had considered.

We had made a nice calendar for the month of December. Every night when the kids went to bed, they got to make a big X on the day that had just passed, so they knew as well as we did what day it was and how long until Christmas.

We were sitting at the kitchen table that Friday morning, discussing the fact that Christmas was less than a week away, when Stan suddenly exclaimed, "What's that?" It was the sound of a low-flying airplane, going right over the cabin. We all ran outside to get a good look, and were very excited when it circled the cabin and dipped its wings at us. It was the mail plane!

"It's such a nice warm day today; do you think we could all go with you?" I asked. "I'm sure we'd have a fun day and not get cold. We've not been out of the cabin in weeks." The temperature was above zero with a slight snow falling.

Stan agreed we could go with him, so I bundled the kids up in their warm clothes, while Stan readied the weasel. He had installed a canvas cover over the entire weasel, and put a nice cushion in the back for the kids to sit on. We were soon on the road. The hours of daylight at that time of the year were quite scarce, so we wanted to take full advantage of all the light that was available.

We had a very uneventful trip into Livengood, traveling along our old friend, the Elliott Highway, although it took us nearly all the daylight hours to get there. It was with a great relief that we picked up the mail, and loaded all those packages into the weasel. Of course, we had to visit with John and Tony at the Livengood Inn. Tony had ordered a turkey (which had just come in on the mail plane), and wanted us to come back for Christmas dinner. He could be very persuasive when he put his mind to it. So, we assured him we'd be back, if the weather didn't turn too cold. Turkey sounded a lot better than the moose roast I'd been planning to cook.

About 4:00 p.m., we loaded the kids back into the weasel to get home with our packages. We got the canvas covering in place, and headed up the hill out of town. By this time, it was quite dark, so we were happy that we had working lights on the weasel. Stan had installed a flexible shaft spotlight, so we were able to shine it wherever we wanted and look for wildlife.

It was a beautiful night as we started out. The weather had finally cleared, and the stars were as bright as diamonds. Periodically, a fiery exhibition of Northern Lights would shoot across the sky in a spectacular display. The temperature had dropped to nearly minus 20°F, but it was nice and toasty warm in the weasel with the canvas cover. The heater put out enough heat that it was nearly too warm under the tarp, and the kids started stripping off their mitts and loosening the zippers on their jackets.

We were slowly making our way up the steep hill coming out of Livengood, with the engine roaring, when suddenly Stan asked with concern, "Do you smell something?"

"Well, yeah, now that you mention it, I do." I replied. "It smells like something *HOT!*"

"We'd better check it out," Stan said. He stopped the weasel, and set the hand brake. We both climbed down from the weasel and followed our noses, to discover that the canvas in the back of the weasel was on fire! Apparently, it had gotten too close to the exhaust pipe. With all the demanding work of climbing up the steep hill, the exhaust pipe had gotten really hot, setting the tarp on fire.

There sat our three little kids in the weasel, snug and happy on their cushion, with their backs against the gas tank; and there was a fire raging just on the other side of the gas tank! I'll tell you, it didn't take us long to rip that canvas off the weasel, and stomp it on the ground.

"Now what do we do?" I asked. "It's too cold for the kids to ride without any heat." The thought also crossed my mind; *it's too cold for me, too!*

"Well, let's get the kids dressed again. We still have some pieces of the canvas left," Stan said. "I'm sure we can patch it back together enough to cover the kids."

It didn't take long for us to wrap the canvas around the kids, but there was no way the heater could be connected to their cocoon. Using the canvas as a windbreak, and huddling together with their clothes zipped again and their mittens back on, the kids stayed warm. That, of course, left Stan and me out in the weather. I was happy to have my parka with its nice wolf fur ruff to pull over my face. I didn't have to watch where we were going. I could leave that for poor Stan. He pulled his parka hood down around his face, too, leaving just a peek hole for his eyes. We both got quite frosty before we reached home, but no frostbite.

We were so very happy to see the cabin looming in the headlights of the weasel. It was a great relief to get into our nice, warm house. The dogs, as always, welcomed us as though we'd been gone for a month. And Santa was a great hit five days later, on Christmas Day. He brought just what the kids had wanted.

The weather was nice on Christmas day, so back to Livengood we went for Christmas dinner. Stan had replaced the canvas tarp on the weasel, and this time, he made sure that it was not close to the exhaust pipe. We had no trouble, either going or coming back home, for which we gave thanks.

It was kind of interesting to walk into Tony's kitchen, and see the turkey sitting on the sideboard, cooling. He had roasted the turkey in his wood burning oven, removed it when it was done, and then put potatoes in the turkey pan in the oven to bake and brown. The turkey was delicious, and so were the potatoes. It was a lovely dinner, and a lovely Christmas – thanks to that mail plane pilot for alerting us to the fact that the mail had arrived. He was a good Santa's helper.

Chapter 16

Duck, Duck, Goose

It had warmed up to about 20°F, which was unusual for a January day in 1964. Stan was readying the weasel to check his trap line. "Do you think we can go with you?" I asked. "It's nice out, and we could do with an outing."

"I don't see why not," he replied. "I've wanted to scout out some more places upriver for beaver trapping in the spring. We can go up the river to the bridge and I can do my scouting, check those traps, and we can come home on the road"

We got the kids dressed in their warm winter coats, boots, scarves, and gloves, and threw in an extra blanket "just in case." We also got some crackers and cheese, and packed a couple bottles of water.

We felt quite adventuresome as we left the cabin in our tracked vehicle. The kids were riding in the back on their nice cushion, with the canvas tarp. Stan and I rode on the seats he'd mounted in the front of the vehicle. We left our regular track where it crossed the river, and blazed a new trail up the frozen Tolovana River.

It was a beautiful day. The sun was shining, and the snow was sparkling like someone had sprinkled it with thousands of diamonds. The only tracks were from wildlife: moose, rabbit, wolf and lynx.

It was fun to travel along the river, skirting the log jams and gravel bars, and the ponds created by them. The entire river was frozen, and covered with a deep layer of snow. It was hard to tell what had made the big ponds. There were snow banks and sculptures in and along the bank, created by the wind. We admired the wonderland; then something looked strange.

"Doesn't that look like fresh water on top of the ice?" I shouted at Stan. The engine of the weasel sat right between the front seats, and it was *noisy*. It really made communication difficult.

"Yeah, it sure does!" he shouted back. "I guess the warm weather started some of the springs running again, and the water's running on top of the ice. But, I don't think we have anything to worry about." Of course, he never did.

"Do you think we ought to turn around?" I yelled.

"No, I'm sure it's just surface water, and won't cause us any trouble," he yelled, as he put the weasel in gear and inched out across the water-covered ice in the river. Sure enough, he was right. There was only about four inches of water on the ice.

At the next gravel bar, we came to another water-covered patch of ice. Without hesitation, we just kept going. Again, we had no trouble. I guessed that maybe Stan *had* been right when he assured me we had nothing to worry about.

But about the sixth such overflowing pond, our good cruising came to an end. We had no sooner gotten onto the pond, when we felt the back end of the weasel settle lower, and it was churning water. It had apparently broken through the ice and into deep water. Stan floored the gas pedal on the weasel, and we crossed that pond like a pontoon boat. The front end of the weasel was on the ice, clawing and crawling, and the ice kept breaking under it. The back end of the weasel was down in the water, shooting a stream of water six-feet high into the air behind us. Stan headed for the shore on the opposite side of the river, and it was with a great sigh of relief that the front track finally caught on solid ground, and pulled the Weasel up out of the water. Behind us, it looked like a frozen lake, with a wide, broken trail of dark water running across it.

"I'm shaking, and I'm not even cold!" yelled Danny. We knew exactly what he meant. I think we were all shaking, but certainly not from the cold.

"I guess we'll just cut across over to the road, and I'll try to scout out the rest of the river another day." Stan said. "We'll park up on the road by the bridge, and I'll check my traps. It won't take more than thirty minutes, and we'll go home on the road."

It only took about twenty minutes to reach the road by the bridge. It was a big relief to be on solid ground once again, on our old friend, the Elliott Highway. No road ever looked so welcoming. Stan turned the weasel around on the road, shut off the engine, and we all breathed a sigh of relief.

"Are you sure you have to check those traps today?" I asked. "I think after all that excitement, maybe we ought to just go on back home. You can come back and check your traps with the snow machine tomorrow, and that way, you won't have to walk to where they are; you can ride the snow machine."

"What a clever idea," he replied. He turned the key on, pushed on the starter, and—nothing.

"So, what's wrong now?" I asked.

"Maybe the battery cable is loose," he replied. "It's under your seat, so move over and I'll check it."

Well, it wasn't the battery cable. The battery was completely dead. For some reason, the alternator had not been charging like it was supposed to, and running the heater had drained the battery.

"What do we do now?" I asked with trepidation. "It's at least four miles to walk home. I don't think the kids could make it, and I'm not sure about me either."

"Well, I guess we could have our lunch." Stan replied. "Probably if the weasel sits for a while, it will start." He sounded reassuring, and I was relieved to notice he *hadn't* said, "Don't worry!"

I handed cheese and crackers to everyone. They really tasted delicious to us, survivors of the black lagoon, so-to-speak.

"Well, here goes!" Stan declared, as he pushed the starter button. Again, nothing happened. It didn't have enough oomph to turn over the engine.

"Now what?" I asked. "It's getting later and later, and if you left now to get the snow machine, it would still take several hours … but that's the only way I can see to get home."

"Well, maybe if I go check my traps now, and we wrap that spare blanket around the battery while I'm gone, it will get enough charge to start the weasel by the time I get back," he said with confidence. I, on the other hand, was anything but confident of this solution.

However, regardless of my thoughts, he wrapped the battery with our spare blanket, strapped on his snowshoes, gathered up his rifle, and strode off along his trail.

That left me with the three kids in the rapidly cooling weasel. And, with no blanket to keep us warm. The battery had our blanket. As I sat there cooling off, I decided that we needed to keep moving to keep the circulation going, and keep ourselves warm.

"Hey, kids!" I said. "How about playing some games? Have you ever played Duck, Duck, Goose?"

They had no idea what I was talking about. "Duck, Duck, Goose? That sounds like something to eat!" Danny exclaimed.

"No, it isn't something to eat. What we need to do is tromp a large circle in the snow, and then tromp in more lines, like spokes in a wheel. I can't remember exactly what we do after that, but I do know that the wolf stands in the middle of the circle, and everyone else runs around the outside, trying to stay away from the wolf. Come on, let's get that circle done!"

As I jumped from the weasel, I found myself in snow that was nearly up to my hips. No wonder Stan had used snowshoes. I noticed that under the bridge there was very little snow, and it was also sheltered from the little breeze that had sprung up.

So, down under the bridge we went, tromping out our "ring" and hollering loudly. I figured that if we made lots and lots of noise, any wildlife that might be in the neighborhood (like the *real* big bad wolf) would give us a wide berth. I know they say that wolves won't attack humans, but I didn't trust those buggers. We had seen quite a collection of wolf tracks.

We were just getting our game going well, when Stan showed up. The kids and I huddled under the bridge, praying that the weasel would start. Climbing into the weasel, Stan said, "Well, I guess there's no time like the present to find out." He removed the blanket from around the battery and pushed the starter. It barely cranked over, but that was all it needed. It fired and the weasel was running. We all shouted with joy to hear that engine roaring.

It was beginning to get dark as we clambered into the weasel. We were happy to see a big, shiny moon peek over the hills. We didn't dare use the lights, with the low battery. We couldn't use the heater either, but we could use the blanket. We lumbered down the Highway at full speed by the light of the moon. The thermometer read minus 10°F when we got home, and it was definitely good to be there.

Chapter 17

Rough Riding Weasel

It was Good Friday, the day the mail plane was due in Livengood, so time to get the mail. For the past several weeks, Stan had been using the snow machine, instead of the weasel, to get the mail. He set several traps along the way, and would check his traps, then go into town for the mail.

This Friday, March 27, 1964, dawned bright, sunny, and *warm*. "Do you think we could go with you today?" I asked. "It's been nearly a month since we've been to town, and it would be good to just get away from the house for a change. And we're having a heat wave. Thirty-five degrees above zero."

"I don't see why not," Stan replied. "We can take the weasel and use the road." He hadn't been on our old friend, the Elliot Highway, for several weeks. Instead, he'd been taking the snow machine on the Green Lightning road across the flat.

"We could always ride in the sled behind the snow machine, if you think that would be better," I replied. "We sort of like that, with our big blanket."

"No, that's *not* a good idea. The snow might be very soft out on the Green Lightning road, and I'd hate to get stuck pulling that heavy sled. I'm sure I'd have no trouble with an empty sled, but with one loaded, we could be in lots of trouble." he replied. *Was he insulting us and our weight?* I never quite decided, so didn't offer any comments.

"Easter is Sunday," I said. "I'll get some goodies to take to John and Tony for Easter." I had baked bread the day before, so I wrapped up a fresh loaf and threw in a few cinnamon rolls, and a couple of hard-boiled, colored eggs. Then it was time to get the kids dressed in their winter clothes. We loaded everything into the weasel, and hit the road. We were moving by 10:00 a.m.

It was a beautiful day as we traveled along. The sun was shining, and the snow was showing signs of melting along the tracks. Water was dripping off some of the trees. We turned onto the Elliott Highway, and had only gone a mile and a half or so, when we found a large glacier blocking the road. Apparently, the warm weather had activated the spring just up the hill from the road, and it had started running again. Of course, the subzero temperatures at night had caused it to freeze, and as luck would have it, it had frozen completely across the road.

"Whoa!" Stan exclaimed. "That sucker looks deep. Look how it slopes away towards the lower edge of the road."

"Do you think we can get over it?" I asked. "Maybe we need to go back, and take the Green Lightning Road across the flat where you've been driving the snow machine."

"I'll go check it out," Stan replied. He jumped down from the weasel, and wandered around on the glacier, looking at it from top to bottom.

Upon his return, he said, "It's only about eight feet deep. I think if I take it slow and easy, I won't have any trouble. You and the kids get out of the weasel, just in case. If something happens, I can always jump out. But don't worry, nothing will happen."

So, with his record of dreadful things happening when he said, "don't worry," I started to worry. We clambered down from the weasel, and huddled along the side of the road, as he gently eased the weasel out onto the pile of ice. He had only gone a short distance, when the weasel started to slide sideways. Having quick reflexes, Stan hit the brake for the upper track, and let the lower track turn him around, so he was no longer sliding sideways. Although it was downright scary to see him go sliding backwards over that eight-foot drop, with his tracks spinning forward and him going backwards.

We raced to the edge of the road. I expected to see the weasel flipped end-over-end, or at the very least, plowed into a tree. Imagine my relief to see it standing calmly right side up, down in the deep snow. It had slid like a toboggan right over the edge of the glacier and come to an easy stop in the snow. And, instead of jumping like he'd promised, Stan had ridden it all the way to the snowbank.

Stan motioned for us to come on down to where he and the weasel were stopped. Since I was the biggest, I broke trail, and it was some trail to break. The wind had drifted the snow along the edge of the glacier, and we were plowing through snow that was nearly thigh high on me. You could hardly see the tops of the kid's heads as they valiantly followed me through the snow. Meanwhile, Stan turned the weasel around, and headed it down the hill towards the flat.

It was a big relief to finally reach the weasel, and crawl aboard. "What happened?" I yelled at him. "I thought you were going to have no trouble. And you said you'd jump if something went wrong."

With a sheepish grin, he replied, "I guess the spring is still running, and there was all this fresh water on top of the ice. I didn't think it would bother when I went walking out there, but then, I've got the studs on my boots. That water sure made the ice slippery. The tracks slid sideways like a sled, so there I went." He never did explain why he had not jumped like he'd promised.

He maneuvered the weasel down through the trees, and onto the old Green Lightning Road. Since he had been on this road most of the winter with his snow machine, we knew there were no pitfalls along it. My only question was, *would the snow be packed enough to hold the heavy weasel?* Yes, it did just fine.

It wasn't very far along the Green Lightning Road until there was a trail that made its way back up the hill and through the tall trees to the Elliott Highway. We took this trail, since he had a trap to check up that way. As we turned onto the Elliott Highway, we saw something black and bulky moving around in the ditch up ahead.

"What do you think that is?" I yelled over the engine noise at Stan.

"Darned if I know," he replied. "I don't have any traps right here, but my lynx trap isn't too far from here. That doesn't look like a lynx, though." As we neared the object, we discovered that it was a wolverine, and boy, was he mad! He was in Stan's trap. Since the trap Stan had set was for lynx, it didn't have a very heavy drag. The wolverine had apparently stopped by to have dinner on Stan's lynx bait, had stepped in the trap, and had dragged the tree that Stan had affixed his trap to for nearly half a mile!

Stan dispatched the wolverine with his trusty .22. "Come look at this," he yelled, as he motioned me out of the weasel. As I gingerly stepped down from the weasel, and looked at the wolverine, I saw that the whole side of his head was missing. Apparently, a hunter had shot him months before during hunting season. That's why he had tried to eat the bait set out for the lynx. The poor critter probably couldn't do much hunting. It was probably a blessing for him to be out of his misery.

We left him lying where he was until our return trip. No predator would bother a wolverine. They are all scared to death of the critters, and with just cause.

We had no more excitement on the way into town. John and Tony were happy to get the goodies, and commented that they had never had colored Easter eggs before. It was good to see other human beings again. We stopped to pick up the wolverine on the way home and made sure we detoured around the glacier. We arrived home just as the stars were appearing in the sky.

When we drove into the yard, we noticed that the wood pile had fallen in. It had been a wet fall, and the top logs on the wood-pile had frozen in a chunk. When Stan was bringing in wood, he'd created a tunnel to get to the dry wood. Now, it was all in a heap.

As we walked into the house, we saw that the globe was off the kerosene lamp. This was unusual, since the cat rarely, if ever, got on top of the piano. Nothing else seemed amiss, though.

After dinner, we turned on the radio. We couldn't believe our ears. The announcer was excitedly talking about damage to Anchorage and then he would switch to what had happened in Seward (giving live reports), then back to Anchorage, Valdez, and Kodiak Island. We looked at each other, perplexed. "What do you think happened?" I asked.

"I wonder if an atomic bomb went off," Stan said, thinking out loud. "No, if that happened, there wouldn't be any radio stations on the air. I have no idea what happened."

We went to bed that night, still wondering and worried. We had no idea what had happened to cause so much destruction, damage and loss of life in

Southeast Alaska. It wasn't until the next morning that we learned from the radio about the Good Friday Earthquake, and how it had devastated Alaska. It remains to this day the largest recorded earthquake in North America, and probably the second largest in the world. We were apparently traveling in the weasel at the time of the earthquake, and that weasel is a very rough ride.

Once we learned about the earthquake, we worried about our friends and neighbors. We felt fortunate that only the wood pile had caved-in and the globe had been knocked off the lamp at our house. However, we knew many people had suffered devastating losses.

Danny with Lady, Red Dog's mother

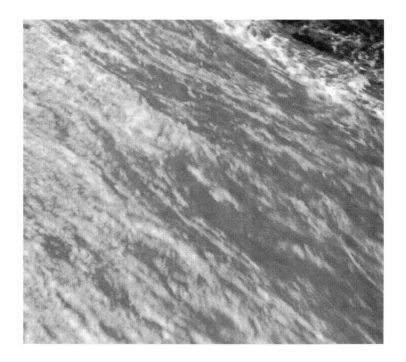

Tolovana River near flood stage

Chapter 18

Treading Water

Stan, the kids, I, and our two dogs climbed into the Weps on that nice sunny day in August 1964 and left our cabin on Wilbur Creek for a few days "vacation" in Fairbanks. The Weps was crowded, with the three kids, and two dogs, but we were going to town, so crowded in happily. We had an uneventful trip down the Elliott Highway to Fairbanks.

We enjoyed visiting with our friends, for the three days we had taken off. We were only slightly concerned about a rather nasty looking accumulation of rain clouds in the direction of the cabin, which hung around all the days we were in town.

Soon the time came for us to return to the cabin. The sun was shining brightly. We gave thanks for the sunshine, and went shopping. We had a lengthy grocery list. We got all our supplies loaded in the Weps, then stopped in at the bulk plant to fill our barrels with diesel and gasoline. Soon we were headed back up the Elliott Highway.

"Do you think there was much rain while we were gone?" I asked Stan.

"I doubt it, it's been a dry summer, so it probably didn't rain at all," he replied, "even though this is about the time the wet weather usually starts. Those clouds were probably just hanging around up here, like they have most of the summer, not doing anything."

Our trip toward home was uneventful, although we did notice that the road was muddy in spots, especially the nearer we got to the cabin. When we arrived at our crossing of the Tolovana River, we were shocked to find it at flood stage. "Good grief!" I said, "Can we drive across? It doesn't look safe to me."

"One feature about the Weps is that it's amphibian, so it's supposed to be able to travel underwater," Stan replied. "I've never tried it, but I think if I put it in low range and four-wheel drive, we'll make it across just fine. We really need to get these barrels of fuel across the river." At least, he hadn't said, "don't worry!"

He put the Weps in its lowest gear, and we gingerly eased our way into the river. It was quite startling to see the river water level with Stan's shoulders in the window on the driver's side. On the downstream side of the Weps, the water level was down below the floorboards. Almost like Moses parting the Red Sea, we inched our way across the river. We thanked our lucky stars that we were loaded so heavily that the current could not take us downriver. We had progressed nearly three-quarters of the way across the river, when the Weps started missing. Soon there was silence—it had died.

"What do we do now?" I asked, as the water started seeping through the door and rising on the floorboards. The one member of our family best equipped to deal with this situation (our Labrador) started whining as he sat in the water. Soon the kids joined in and started whimpering as they looked at the threatening water on the driver's side of the Weps.

"This Weps has a 24-volt system," Stan replied. "I think we can make it out of the river using just the starter." He pushed on the starter and with the Weps in low gear, it did move. It gradually ground its way out of the river, with a stream of water pouring out behind it.

"Now what?" I asked, relieved to have made it that far.

"Now we hoof it to the cabin," Stan said. "Hopefully I can get that coil dried out on the Weps before we need to leave here again. Anyway, I think it's the coil that got wet. The Weps isn't as waterproof as it's supposed to be."

It was the coil, and within a few days, the coil dried out, Stan put it back in the Weps, and it was purring like a kitten. In about ten days, the river dropped enough so that we could drive across without any trouble.

Bloom family at the mine, 1965 from l-r: Debbie, Henry, Betty, Dad and Mom.

Chapter 19

Henry and the Road Grader

It was August of 1965, and my Dad, my Mom, and three siblings were visiting from Montana. The entire extended family spent most of the summer at the mining claims, but in late August we decided we should move back to North Pole. Stan had just gotten a job working for Civil Service at Eielson Air Force Base, and it was time to get Danny and Sue enrolled in school. Besides, we had several fix-it projects that needed to be done before we could be comfortable at our house in North Pole. Our renters had moved, so our house was empty. Soon Mom and Dad would be going back to Montana.

All of us had spent the weekend at the cabins near Livengood, and it was our intention to spend the entire week in North Pole, working on the house. However, both Stan and I had forgotten to shut-off a valve in our water pipeline at the mine – he thought it was me that had forgotten (and I was sure it was him!); since it had started raining, we didn't want the pipeline to wash out. Thus, Henry and I found ourselves on the Elliott Highway headed north to remedy the situation.

We left after dinner on a Wednesday, and since Alaska has many hours of daylight in August, it was still daylight when we reached our access road. As we rounded the corner, the first word out of our mouths was, "Whoa!" There, sitting smack dab in the middle of our access road, was a State of Alaska yellow road grader.

It would be about a mile-long hike to the cabin from that point, if we had to walk. And, between us and the cabin was the mosquito-infested flat. Neither Henry nor I looked forward to trying to walk across that. Besides, there might be bears about, and we didn't even have a rifle. We had ourselves one big problem – how to get around the grader. It was parked so that it was impossible to detour it!

"What do we do now?" Henry asked. Jokingly, I said, "You get up in it, start it, and move it." Henry was just 12-years-old. I was flabbergasted when he jumped out of the truck, crawled up into the grader, and it actually started. It was a bit hairy finding a gear that went forward, but he did, and soon had it pulled far enough off the road so that I could maneuver past with our truck.

"I suppose we ought to put it back where it came from," I yelled at him, after I'd squeezed past in our truck. "I wouldn't want the road folks to know we'd moved it." He managed to find a reverse gear, and backed it almost to the spot where it had been. Then came the next big problem – how to shut the thing off. He tried this and that, pulled every knob and lever he could find, and still it kept running. Finally, he found a lever under the seat, and we were blessed with silence. We continued on our merry way, thanking our lucky stars as a horde of hungry mosquitoes flew around the truck when we were crossing the flat.

We discovered that we were too late to stop a wash-out on the pipeline. But, we did the best we could to detour the water away from the wash out, and were very happy to fall into bed late that night, completely exhausted. Early the next morning found us back in the truck headed towards Fairbanks, and guess what?

Unsurprisingly, the road grader was right where Henry had left it. But, this time there was an even bigger problem. It refused to start. It wouldn't even turn over. After talking it over, we decided that the battery was probably dead. Maybe one of those switches Henry had tried, when trying to shut the thing off, had been connected to the lights or something else electrical, and had drained the battery.

Henry had just gotten down from the grader, and we were contemplating whether or not we could attach the jumper cables from our truck to the battery of the road grader, when what should drive up but an orange State of Alaska pickup, with two guys in it.

They got out of their pickup. The big, mean looking one looked at us, and charged, "Have you been messing around with this road grader?"

Looking as innocent as I could, I replied, "Do I look like someone that could start a road grader? But, this is a private road, our access road, and you have no business parking that machine on our road. Get it out of the way, will you?"

He crawled up into the grader, and was not happy when it would not turn over. We were not surprised, but tried to act like we were!

The other guy with him said, "Remember last week the battery went dead, too? There must be a short in it or something." Aha, we thought, so maybe it was not Henry's tinkering after all that drained the battery.

"How am I supposed to get out of here?" I asked. "I need to get back to Fairbanks." I was happy they didn't ask how I'd gotten there in the first place!

"I have an axe in the truck, and I think if I cut down a few of these trees, you can get around," said the big, burly guy. "I'm awfully sorry Ma'am. We just didn't think anyone was using this road."

He dug out his axe, and cut down a couple of trees. We did make our way around the grader, and were soon on our way back to Fairbanks.

The next weekend, we were happy to find that grader gone.

Outcropping of Rocks along the Elliott Highway
known to us as "Dad's Rocks"

Chapter 20

Dad's Rocks

Sometimes the kids would get sleepy during our numerous trips up and down the Elliott Highway, and "take a short cut," which meant they would have a nap. Other times we'd sing. We had quite a repertoire of songs, from Old McDonald Had a Farm, to My Old Kentucky Home. At other times, we'd play "I spy," and try to be the first to see something out of the ordinary, like perhaps a tree, or a white rock, or perhaps another car.

One day in September 1966, we were on our way back to the cabin from North Pole. As we traveled over the Elliott Highway, we marveled at the golden pathway that our road had become. The birch trees had shed their leaves, and the entire road was paved with gold colored leaves. This was a beautiful sight.

We were coming down the hill after reaching the top of Wickersham Dome, and in front of us was a whole hillside strewn with huge rocks and boulders, amid the yellow leaves. I said to the kids, "See those rocks up there? Your Dad put them there."

The questions flew hot and heavy. "Why?" asked Danny.

"He was bored," I replied.

"How did he get them there?" asked Sue.

"He used his bulldozer, and put them right there where you see them."

About that time, Stan got involved with the story, and told the kids some long involved yarn about having nothing better to do, and having all those rocks in the front yard of the house, so he'd just decided to put them on the hillside. That way, everyone traveling the Elliott Highway could enjoy seeing them. By the time he finished with the yarn, we had passed the rocks, and were well on our way to another jumble of rocks.

"Did you put those rocks there, too, Dad?" Sue asked.

"No," Stan replied. "Someone else must have put those there." This particular rock formation is named Grapefruit Rocks. Maybe a Mr. Grapefruit one day was bored?

I sort of forgot about this conversation until the next time we were traveling along the same route, and one of the kids pointed out, proudly, that Dad had put those rocks there. And, every time we passed, one or another of the kids would comment about Dad's pile of rocks.

Eventually, the kids quit talking about "Dad's Rocks" when we drove by, and I had forgotten all about it. It was many years later, when the kids had invited a playmate to spend some time at the mine, I was quite amazed when they retold the story of how their Dad had put those rocks there. The playmate was a little skeptical, but the kids were very convincing about it being a true story; they soon had the playmate convinced, too.

To this day, that area is known to our family as Dad's Rocks. Although, you will never find it on any official map.

The Gray Ghost, with Stan, Rose, Sue, Sallie and
Cyndi

Chapter 21

Sylvester

This is not a funny or happy tale, but in memory of Sylvester, it should be told. It was the fall of 1972, and we were in the process of moving our menagerie from our mining cabin back to our North Pole home. This was our semi-annual pilgrimage. In the spring after school was out for the summer, we would load up our dogs, cats, and farm animals, and move everything to the cabin.

In the fall, we would do the reverse; load up everything, and move back to North Pole. On this particular move, Stan was driving the Weps, while I was driving the Gray Ghost (we had replaced our Mercury car with a 1965 International Carry-all, and my sister Betty had dubbed it the "Gray Ghost"). Stan had the dogs in the Weps, while I had the kids and cats in the Ghost.

By this time, we had three cats. Two of them had been with us for several years, but the newest addition to the household was Sylvester. He was just a kitten, born in the spring. He was black and white, and had a black spot on his chin which reminded us of Sylvester in the funny papers. Therefore, his name was Sylvester. He and Sue bonded immediately, and were nearly inseparable.

We were finally loaded into our various vehicles, and off we went. It was always rather sad to say goodbye to our cabin for the winter, but it was exciting to move back into our house, with electric lights, telephone, and running water. With sad faces, we made the trip across the river, and traversed the tundra flat. We had a cable across our access road, so it took us a while to get both vehicles on the outside of it, and get it locked behind us.

"I think I'll stop in the gravel pit, and check on my load. Do you want to just keep going, or do you want to deliver me a cup of coffee?" Stan said, with a twinkle in his eye.

"I can get you some coffee," I dutifully replied. "I think both thermoses got packed into the Gray Ghost."

I pulled into the gravel pit behind Stan. The girls planned to stay in the Gray

Ghost and wait until I'd made my delivery. Sue was in the front seat, holding Sylvester on her lap. He was purring, and seemed very content.

I got out of the Ghost, picked up the thermos of coffee and a cup, and just as I slammed the door, Sylvester made a gigantic leap off Sue's lap. His head collided with the closing door with a sickening crunch. And poor Sylvester was lying there, squirming and kicking on the ground.

The girls started wailing, I started wailing, and Stan came running up to see what the ruckus was all about. Mumbling something under his breath about weeping women and damned cats, he went to the Weps, got a shovel, and gathered up the now lifeless body of poor Sylvester. He buried him right there in the gravel pit. It was a long time before the girls forgave me for "murdering" Sylvester, if they ever have. They apparently had the idea that I had done it on purpose. And, sometimes, even to this day, they will remind me of the day I murdered Sylvester.

Sylvester

Chapter 22

A Taunting Moose

It was the day after the close of moose season, that September of 1973. We had a disappointing season that year, and had not found a bull moose. We drove our car to the mine late Friday night, and were on our way home late Sunday night in the dark. It seemed like the work was never done at the mine, and we had worked all weekend getting the place ready for winter. Stan was very tired from all his toiling, so I was the "designated driver." The snowplows had been out, and a berm of snow about three feet high defined the edges of the road.

As we drove up the steep hill after crossing the Tatalina River, I was a little concerned about the slippery, snow-covered road. Fortunately, we had no problem. We had reached an area where the road flattened out, when ahead in the car lights, we spotted a large animal.

"Mom, look!" shouted our daughter Sue, "isn't that a moose?"

"Boy, it sure looks like one," I replied, "and look at the size of that rack."

This brought Stan upright and wide awake. He was wishing it was still moose season, and daylight. That moose was a big one, all right, and was ambling along on our side of the road, taking his own sweet time. "You'd better slow down," Stan warned. "You don't dare go around him ... what if he decided to charge the car while you were passing? You better just hang back here and wait for him to leave the road."

I did as I was instructed, and we followed him at a slow pace for what seemed like forever, but probably was only a thousand feet or so. Then, he came to a sudden stop in the road, and looked at us over his shoulder. We also came to a stop. The suspense reminded me of tales of the showdown at the O. K. Corral. Then, he slowly turned and started toward us.

"Put it in reverse!" Stan yelled. And, that's exactly what I did. We backtracked down the road at about the same pace we'd just come up it.

"What do we do, Mom, if he charges us?" Sue asked.

I replied, "Well, we'd just hope we can outrun him."

"Going backwards?" Sue asked in disbelief. "I don't think you back up so good." I must admit that a slight doubt of my backing-up abilities did cross my own mind.

"Look, he turned around, and is going back up the hill!" shouted Sue with relief. "Let's go." And off we went, following him back up the hill. Our caravan went past where he had turned around before, and on around another corner. We kept our distance, but could easily see him in the headlights. Imagine our surprise when he again stopped, turned around and started back towards us.

"Put it in reverse," Sue sang out. She didn't have to be so insistent because we were in reverse and backing up before she got the words out of her mouth.

Back around the corner, and down the hill we went, keeping a good eye out for both the road and the moose. He just kept coming, right toward our headlights.

"Try honking the horn," Stan suggested. "That might scare him off the road, or, you could try flashing the lights."

"Are you sure that won't just make him mad?" I asked. "I don't think it's a good idea when I'm going backwards. You know, I never did learn to drive very well backwards, Sue is right."

Sure enough, at about the same place in the road, old Mr. Moose turned around. *Now,* I thought, *now is the time to try to scare him.* So, there we were; honking, flashing, and slowly following this massive bull-moose down the road. He must have been both blind and deaf, because he paid absolutely no attention to our noise and lights. He just lowered his head, and ambled down the road.

About halfway between his first and second turn-around places, he once again turned around, and began sauntering toward us. By now, we were pretty well programmed so that when he turned, we immediately stopped and started backing up.

"I wonder how much gas we have?" asked Stan. "At this rate, we could be here all night."

"I just hope he doesn't go any faster than he has been," I said. "As it is, he's moving faster than I want to back up. It's hard to tell where to go in the dark. And, if he pushes us into backing down that steep hill to the Tatalina River, I doubt we can get traction enough to get going again until we'd backed all the way down."

Backwards we went again, around the corner, and down the small hill once more. It seemed to me that the moose had stepped up his pace, and was coming at us faster than before. About the time we reached the place we'd stopped the time before, he suddenly lunged over the snow berm and disappeared into the darkness.

Why don't things like that ever happen during hunting season?

Bull Moose along highway in summer
Could this be our moose?

Chapter 23

Salmon and Graham Crackers

My brother Henry returned to Alaska in 1973. He had moved to Montana with my parents and sisters about ten years before. He attended school there, graduated from high school, went to Chefs School, and worked one summer on a dude ranch in Wyoming. Then, he decided to move back to Alaska. He was living with us while he got settled. He was working at the Pancake House in Fairbanks.

He returned to our home from his early morning shift one Friday in March 1974, and Stan asked him if he'd like to take a ride the next day to the mine. Stan was busily hauling barrels of diesel to the mine for our summer's work. Henry said he would enjoy going with Stan.

On Saturday morning, shortly after breakfast, they began getting the truck ready for their trip up the Elliott Highway. This involved: loading the barrels; making sure the truck was full of gas; checking the oil; checking the air pressure in the tires, and filling the water can. In the meantime, I prepared their lunch. I packed sandwiches made from the leftovers of a moose roast we'd had for dinner, chips, and some cinnamon rolls that I'd baked the day before. I also dug out several bags of things I wanted them to leave at the mine. These boxes contained such things as clothing, flour and cornmeal, a can or two of smoked salmon, and some miscellaneous odds and ends.

When the guys finished with their outdoor chores, Henry asked, "Are we ready to roll?"

"Not quite," Stan replied, "we'd better pick up those sacks of things that Rose wants us to take to the mine, and get our lunch."

They trooped into the house, and started grabbing the stack of plastic bags and boxes I had set aside. About the time they were starting to carry things, Cyndi (our youngest daughter), cut herself on a piece of paper, so I was in the bathroom doing first aid, when they hollered, "goodbye!" And, they were off.

When I emerged from the bathroom, I was surprised to see they'd missed a bag

... and upon checking, I discovered that it was their lunch. I thought about loading the kids in the car, and seeing if I could catch them, but decided it was hopeless. Hopefully, they could find something to eat at the cabin. I silently wished them luck.

"We have to stop at the bulk plant to get gas," Stan told Henry. "Then, we can head up the Highway to the mine." They soon were loaded with fuel, and on their way.

They had not gone very far on the Elliott, when Henry hollered, "Hey, look at that!" And there in the middle of the road was a beautiful cow moose, with twin calves. The calves didn't look like they were more than a few days old. As the truck drew near to the moose, she seemed in no hurry to get her family off the road. Stan was forced to nearly stop as he waited for the moose family to amble off the road. Soon there was a break in the snow berm, and the moose family strolled off the road.

The rest of the trip to the mine was uneventful. Stan had been there several days earlier with a load of diesel and had parked at the road. He had hiked into the cabin on his snowshoes, started the bulldozer and plowed the road all the way to the Elliott Highway. He then had to hike back to get the truck and its load. So, the road into the cabin was in very good condition.

Once they reached the cabin, Stan said, "You get a fire going in the stove, and I'll unload these barrels. I'm starved, and can't wait for lunch."

So, Henry got some kindling and started a roaring fire in the barrel stove, while Stan unloaded the barrels. Stan backed the truck up to his stockpile, and using an old rimless tire, he pushed a barrel off the tailgate of the truck, which landed in the middle of that old tire. Then, he'd jump down, stand the barrel up, and "walk" it into position. It took him a while to get the truck unloaded, but before too long, he drove back to the cabin.

Henry helped unload the bags of supplies, and they were ready to dig into their lunch. They looked in the first bag, then another, and another. They checked out each box, and were quite appalled when they found no lunch. They did manage to find a can of smoked salmon, but nothing to eat with it.

"Let me see if I can find some crackers we may have left from last year," Stan said. He looked, but the only thing that remotely resembled a cracker was a box of cinnamon flavored graham crackers.

"Ugh, smoked salmon and cinnamon graham crackers. That doesn't sound very appetizing," Stan said, "but it's better than nothing." So, they opened the can of salmon, opened the graham crackers, and ate everything. After a short rest, it was time to get back in the truck and head for Fairbanks. After an uneventful trip without seeing a taunting moose or a moose family, they rolled into the yard.

The first thing out of both of their mouths was, "Where's our lunch?"

I had to admit to them that when we found it (still sitting where I'd put it for them to load), the girls and I had eaten it for *our* lunch. We may even have bragged about how delicious it was. For some reason, they blamed *me* for having hidden it—in plain sight — forcing them to live off the land, so-to-speak. I argued it was their own fault for being so careless with their packing. Who was right?

Snow covered Tolovana River

Chapter 24

No Trustworthy Drivers

The year was 1974, and our good friends Bob and Dee and the five of us (Stan, Sallie, Sue, five-year-old Cyndi, and I) decided to go to our cabin at the mine for the weekend. Stan and I loaded our camping supplies, which included our snow machine and the toboggan (along with some heavy quilts) into the Gray Ghost and set off one Saturday morning in the month of February. While the thermometer was hovering around the 20°F mark, the sun was shining, and the sky was blue.

We were to meet Bob and Dee at the Fox Spring, where we could fill our water jugs with good spring water. It was great to find them waiting for us, and all ready to go. Bob and Dee had their snow machine on a small trailer, while ours was in the back of the Weps. We filled our water cans, and took off down the road. The Elliott Highway was snow-packed, and still had lots of heavy traffic from the construction of the Trans-Alaska Pipeline. We had to dodge big trucks and smaller pickups, but we made it to the gravel pit that the highway crews had cleared of snow, where we could park our vehicles. (This was the burial site of Sylvester, Sue's beloved cat.)

We got the snow machines unloaded, and all our goodies loaded on them and the toboggan, and were ready to travel down our access road to the cabin.

"Cyndi, who do you want to ride with?" I asked. She replied, after pondering for a while, "I'll ride with you on the toboggan."

I got myself settled on the toboggan, along with Sue and Cyndi, and we wrapped up in a heavy quilt to keep us warm. Not only were we wrapped up in it, but it was under us to keep us warm, and it was pulled over our legs to keep any snow off. The supplies were behind us. We were as snug as bugs in a rug. Sallie opted to ride with Stan on the snow machine.

We set off on our access road with Stan driving the snow machine, pulling the toboggan, and following Bob and Dee who were breaking trail with their snow machine. Since we had quite a bit of food and water on the toboggan, plus the three of us, it was fairly heavy. This required the snow machine to huff and puff at times.

If you recall, our access road to the mine was a little over a mile in length, running through spruce and fir covered uplands for a short distance. Then, it dropped down a short, but steep hill, with a sharp curve, before it entered a muskeg flat. The flat was about a half mile across, with water running down the road in the summer, and then the road meandered through some tall fir trees near the river crossing.

Can you imagine what happened next? Coming down the hill, the heavy toboggan crashed into the snow machine. When we hit the corner, we in our snug blanket, didn't make the turn. We flew right off the toboggan and into a deep snowbank, blanket, food, and all. Stan just kept going on the snow machine. Cyndi, who was the youngest and in the front of the toboggan, ended up buried headfirst in the snowbank. It wasn't long before Stan realized there was a problem, stopped, and came back to extricate Cyndi from the snowbank. Sue and I were still struggling to get out from our snug cocoon made from our big blanket.

Cyndi was not one bit happy when he pulled her out of the snowbank, and screamed at the top of her lungs. Once she calmed down, she hollered, "I don't want to ride with you anymore!" Thinking she had a point, we agreed that she could ride with Bob and Dee. They had returned to see what the problem was and were going to continue breaking trail for the rest of us.

Before we got off the flat, guess what? Yes, they ran off the road, and upset their snow machine, sending Cyndi into another snowbank headfirst. You could have heard her ten miles away.

Bob pulled her out of the snowbank this time, and we hurried as fast as we could to the cabin, before she became a victim of frostbite. It didn't take us long, once we got to the cabin, to have a roaring fire. Cyndi had finally settled down and was enjoying the heat ... until Sallie yelled, "Look at Cyndi!" And, sure enough, she'd gotten too close to the red-hot barrel stove, and the back side of her snow machine suit was melting. Sallie grabbed her, and started whacking on the hot spot. (Sallie always looked for any excuse to spank Cyndi.) The suit was completely melted on the backside. It was a good thing we had some old clothes at the cabin, so she could get back to Fairbanks without freezing her behind.

But Cyndi was torn when trying to decide which snow machine she wanted to ride on back to the pickups. It was an uneventful return to the vehicles and on back to town. The trusty Elliott did not toss her into a snowbank.

Stan and Bob with snow machine

Chapter 25

Houndi Disappears

In 1974, we had a seven-year-old female beagle named Houndi. She had been a gift from a good friend. We had only had her for a year or so, so she was still a fairly new addition to our family

One bright and sunny day in early April, we loaded up the Weps with supplies, and were making a weekend trip to the mine. It was such a beautiful day, that Sue and Sallie asked if they could pull down the benches in the Weps, and ride in the pickup box. They were tired of sharing the small front seat with the two dogs, and the rest of us. Since it was such a pretty day, we let them. And, they wanted Houndi to ride with them in the back of the Weps, so we allowed that, too.

We took several five-gallon plastic water cans with us, hoping the river would still be frozen so we could drive across it to the cabin, and not have to tote the water cans across the foot bridge. After all, the ice hadn't gone out on the Tanana River yet, and usually the Tolovana River breakup occurred sometime after the Tanana. As was our habit, we stopped at the Fox Spring to fill our water cans before venturing up our old friend, the Elliott Highway.

Sue and Sallie jumped down from the back of the Weps once we'd stopped at the spring. "Be careful," I cautioned. "Don't get too close to that running water, or you may slide into the stream. That snow looks slippery."

They were careful, and soon Stan had the water cans filled and secured in the Weps. "Time to go," he called to the girls. They came running down the trail, and climbed into the Weps. I was just getting into the front seat, when there was a powerful yell from the back. Sallie was jumping around like she had ants in her pants. She was hollering and crying, while Sue looked on in stupefaction. What could possibly have happened?

"A wasp bit me on the butt when I sat down," Sallie gasped. "Ohhhhh, it hurts!"

Usually for a wasp sting, we would put a paste of baking soda and water on it, and that seemed to remove the worst of the pain from the sting ... but what does one do when you are miles away from any baking soda? We gave her an aspirin, but that was about all the first-aid supplies we had. Then, the next question was, how was she to ride with a stung posterior?

We finally rigged up some books under her, so that the stung part was not touching the seat, and headed for the mine. We had gone about a mile, when Cyndi said, "Where's Houndi?" And, sure enough, Houndi was missing.

"She must still be back at the spring. I didn't know she'd even got out of the back of the pickup," Stan said. "We'll turn around and go get her."

It was easy to turn the Weps around, and soon we were headed back towards the spring. We kept looking and looking, but could not find Houndi. She had vanished. And, as we stopped near the spring and looked closely at the snow along the side of the road, we could see her foot prints where she had tried to follow us. Not far down the road, there was a car track that pulled over, and Houndi's tracks disappeared. Apparently, someone had stopped and picked her up, and we never saw her again.

When we got to the mine, the river was in no condition to drive across since the ice had gone out early. We ended up having to haul the water cans across the foot bridge after all. All in all, that was not a good trip.

Houndi

Chapter 26

A Slick Spot in a Bad Place

"Brring. Brring." The phone was always ringing when I had my hands in the dishwater. Grabbing a towel and drying my hands, I answered the phone. I was surprised when a masculine voice I didn't recognize asked, "Is this Rose?"

After I assured him that it was, he said, "I don't want to worry you, but your husband has had an accident. He's just fine. And so are your brother, and the dog. I pulled his van back onto the Elliott, but he had a couple of flat tires. I dropped the tires off at the Big Bend Tire Shop, and they ought to be fixed in an hour or so. Stan wants you to bring them to him. He's at about mile 40 on the Elliott Highway, but you won't have any trouble finding him. He can't go anywhere without those tires. He's in a nice, wide spot in the road."

I was pretty flabbergasted with that news. Stan, my brother Henry, and our beagle Jeffrey had left early that morning in February 1975, to take a load of diesel fuel to the mine. They were driving the old Gray Ghost, our 1965 International panel truck. I was expecting them to be home in time for supper, but that was apparently not to be.

The girls would be home from school in about half an hour, so I got some sandwiches put together, and got ready for our unexpected trip. When the girls came home, I gave them the news that we were going up the Highway. After hearing everyone was all right, they were very excited, because this beat having to do homework. They quickly changed their clothes, and we all got into the car.

The tires were ready to be picked up, and while they didn't fit into the trunk very well, we managed to tie the trunk lid shut, and off we went. The road was snow-packed, but it wasn't overly slippery. We speculated all the way there as to how Stan had managed to run off the road. Also, we knew that the spot around Mile 40 was a hill, with an extensive drop off on the lower side. But, we kept assuring ourselves that the truck driver said they weren't hurt.

As we got to Mile 40, sure enough, there was the Ghost sitting in a wide spot in the road. It was getting dark by that time, so we couldn't see where it had gone off the road.

Stan and Henry were happy to see us, and very happy to have the sandwiches. "What happened?" I asked.

"We were coming down the hill, and everything was fine, until we hit a spot on the road where a truck had apparently spilled a bunch of fuel," Stan replied. "When we hit that, the Ghost just swung around and around, and on one of the rounds, guess what happened to us? We headed right over the cut-bank. Luckily, we headed straight down it, and there is a little shelf down about thirty feet where the snow was piled quite deeply; enough to stop us, or we'd have been headed on down to the river."

My brother Henry piped up with, "Rosie, you ought to have heard those barrels bouncing around in the Ghost. They made so much noise, that Jeffery and I were scared to death. Let me tell you, when that van stopped, I was out the door, and crawling up the bank in a hurry. You never saw a fat boy move so quickly! And

Jeffrey was right on my heels. We beat Stan up the hill."

"We were very lucky," Stan added. "I checked the Ghost out, and the only damage I could see was that both of the front tires were flat. I guess they got punctured on the rocks, or maybe just got the wind knocked out of them. We were also lucky that trucker stopped, and had a winch. He hooked onto us, and winched us right back onto the road, and then he dragged us over to this wide spot. He even waited until I could get the tires off, and then took them in for us to the tire shop. He sure was a nice guy."

It didn't take very long after the sandwiches were devoured to get the tires back on the Ghost. As Stan had surmised, there was nothing wrong with the vehicle. It ran like a top the rest of the way home.

Chapter 27

A Lot of Trouble for One Box

You know what they say about the Merry Month of May? Well, it wasn't being so very merry for us. We had all settled into our 1964 Ford car after work and school one Friday evening in 1975, and headed up the Highway towards our mine. There had been quite a few trucks on the road after we left the paved part of the Highway, and we had been forced to wait in one place for several hours while one of the big trucks bearing pipes for the Trans-Alaska Pipeline was pulled out of the ditch. This put us into the mine about midnight.

The following morning, after a hearty breakfast of moose steak and fried potatoes, we were sitting around the table, enjoying a second cup of coffee, when Stan said, "Where's that box that has the parts for the pump in it? I don't think I saw it."

I was shaken, and replied, "Didn't you put it in the car? Isn't it in the trunk?"

Sue chimed in with, "Sallie and I unloaded the trunk this morning while you were cooking breakfast, and I don't remember seeing it." With a sinking heart, we all trooped out the door looking for the box ... which of course, was nowhere to be seen.

"What do we do now? I asked. The whole purpose of this trip was to get the pump ready for the upcoming season. Stating the obvious, I said, "You need the parts in that box to fix the pump."

With a thoughtful look on his face, Stan replied, "Well, I could go ahead and take it apart, and you could run back into town and get the box." His idea was that we could still get the pump fixed before we had to go home the next day.

While I wasn't overly excited by this idea, it did seem to be a solution, and I couldn't think of anything better. "Okay," I said, "I'll do it ... anyone want to come with me?"

My question met with dead silence. Even our six-year-old had things she wanted to do at the mine. "Oh, Mom," pleaded Sue, "Can't we stay and clean Pete's house? You know, you said we could sleep in it all summer, and we want to get it fixed up." I *had* promised them they could sleep in that house. It was only a few yards from our house, and had been occupied by an old- timer named "Pete" one summer, hence its name.

"Well, I guess you can stay, but you have to do the dishes, since I want to get on the road," I told the girls, "and, I expect dinner to be ready when I get back." This was okay with them, so by 10:00 a.m., I was on my way to town.

I had no trouble on my way into town. I did notice that a lot of the trucking companies were stockpiling their trailers at the top of Wickersham Dome, at about 27 Mile on the Elliott Highway. Apparently, the road restrictions were about to go into effect during break-up, and they wanted to get as much hauled to the end of the pavement as possible. It was getting to be quite a log jam in the large parking area on top of the hill.

I found the box sitting on the table where we had left it so it would be in plain sight and we wouldn't forget it. After running a couple of other errands, I was back on the road by 3:00 p.m. I figured I'd just make it back to the mine in time for dinner. I knew exactly what we would be having for dinner. I had only taken enough food for the weekend and the four meals we'd have while there. And, I was surely hoping the girls had remembered to put the moose roast in the oven. It would taste pretty good when I got home.

I was making my way up a hill about thirty miles from Fairbanks when suddenly, I heard a "clunk," and the engine started racing. The worst part was that the car was slowing down. I put in the clutch, eased off on the gas, and slowly came to a stop on the side of the road. Now what had happened? I tried to put the car into low, and while it seemed like it went into gear, the car would not move. The engine would just race. I could coast down the hill in reverse, but that wasn't much help. I wanted to go the other way!

So, there I sat, not quite halfway between Fairbanks and the mine! And, calling upon my great mechanical know-how, I decided that the car's clutch had probably gone out. I decided that it wouldn't do much good if I got a ride to the mine, since we didn't have any other vehicle there. So, the best thing to do was to hitch a ride into Fairbanks, and pick up our Weps. There were lots and lots of trucks coming back down the road after leaving their trailers at 27 Mile, so it was an easy job to flag down a truck and catch a ride.

When we got to Fairbanks, the trucker dropped me at the first gas station we came to, per my request. I immediately called my faithful friend, Betty. I was one happy camper when she answered the phone. "Betty!" I exclaimed, "Are you busy?" (Talk about a leading question.)

"I'm just getting ready to take Ralph his dinner, since he's working swing shift this week," she replied. "Why? What's up – I thought you were at the mine this weekend?"

I explained what had happened, and asked if she could give me a ride out to the Weps in North Pole. "I don't know how to ask you this," I continued, "but I really don't like to leave the car beside the road all week end, either! Do you think we could get it and pull it home? I could probably still make it back to the mine late this evening."

"I don't know why not," she replied. "I'll bring Jimmy, and he can steer the car while you tow it. He's good at that, and he knows how to keep the tow-rope taut. You and I can pull him with the Weps." Jimmy, at the age of twelve, was more than willing to drive the car. He thought it would be great fun.

In about twenty minutes, Betty and Jimmy showed-up at the gas station where I was waiting and we all clambered into her pickup for the twelve mile drive out to our home in North Pole. The Weps started on the first try, and we all settled into the cab and headed back toward the car.

We were about half a mile from where the car was sitting, when we heard a loud bang. "What was that?" Jimmie asked.

"Darned if I know, but something is wrong." I replied, as the Weps kind of skewed from side to side.

Stopping, we got out and looked. Wouldn't you know? The back tire on the driver's side had blown. "We should be able to get this changed in a jiffy," I said.

After getting the jack in exactly the right position, we got the Weps jacked up enough to take off the tire, but that stubborn tire refused to budge. "Hey, come and look at this," I said, "that split rim has somehow gotten itself hooked over the brake drum, and it won't come off." Instead of having a normal tire rim, for some reason the tires on the Weps had a split rim, and boy, was that sucker "split."

We used screwdrivers, the lug wrench, and anything we could find, but could not pry that split rim off the brake drum. We were quite relieved when a truck pulled up behind us, and the driver jumped down from the cab.

"What seems to be the trouble, Ma'am?" he asked. Upon being shown the problem, he confidently offered to get his big hammer and pry bar from the truck. "Just what we needed," I thought. So, off he went, and soon returned with the tools in hand.

Whap! Whap! Whap! He hit that rim for all he was worth, but it refused to budge. After trying for about fifteen minutes, he finally said, "Ma'am, I'm sorry, but I have to get this load up the hill. I'll stop on my way back, and see if we can't get that thing apart. If not, I can give you a ride into town, and you can get a wrecker."

"I have an idea," I told him. "What do you think about taking the winch cable, running it up around one of those trees in front of us, back around this tree that's just opposite the wheel, and hooking it to the tire? Do you think that would work?"

"Ma'am," he said, "I don't think so. For one thing, you'd have to watch out for traffic, or you might catch someone. For another, I don't think the winch could pull that rim off. No, Ma'am, you just wait here, and I'll stop on my way back, and I'm sure we can get it off when I have more time."

As he drove off, I had a sinking feeling in the pit of my stomach. Stan and I only had two vehicles, and here they both were, broken down on the road about half a mile from each other, and thirty miles from Fairbanks.

"Well," I told Betty, "I think my idea is worth a try. Don't worry. Once we get it hooked up, you can watch for traffic from one direction, and Jimmy can watch for it from the other. I don't see why the winch won't pull that tire right off. (Did I, myself, just say "don't worry?")

Setting to with gusto, we soon had the winch cable stretched across the road, around a tree, back to the other tree, and hooked up to the tire. Not a car or truck had passed us while we worked. "Are we ready?" I called.

"Yes," came back the response, "Let her rip!"

About the time the cable was starting to get tight, down the hill came a truck. "Truck coming!" Betty yelled. I quickly dropped the cable to make it slack so we wouldn't "catch him," like our trucker friend had prophesied.

For the next ten minutes or so, we went through the same rigmarole ... tighten up the cable until all the slack was gone, then hurry to loosen it because a vehicle was coming from one direction or another. As the tenth car flew down the hill, it pulled to a stop near where Betty was watching for traffic. The driver jumped out, and, after conferring with Betty, he came staggering down the hill toward me.

"Here, let me do that!" he shouted. "I can get that tire off for you." But, I noticed (as had Betty) that he was about three sheets to the wind, and barely able to stand. Just the kind of help we didn't need.

"You know what we *really* need?" I asked him. "We need someone to go way up the hill, and stop some of those cars before they get here."

"I'm your man," he proudly announced, and set off in a weaving pattern for his assigned spot.

"Okay, it looks clear" Betty yelled.

As I tightened up the cable, I said a little prayer that this scheme would work. The cable tightened, the Weps rocked sideways a bit, there was suddenly a loud bang and thump, and the tire was off.

"Drop the cable," Betty yelled, "our 'friend' has let one get through!" And sure enough, over the hill came a car going like a bat out of Hell … right over our cable that was nearly slack, and on down the road it sped

We were happy to see that the speeding car hadn't caught the cable or run over our intoxicated friend. With our thanks, he got into his car and made his way on down the road. We had just about finished tightening the lug nuts on the spare tire, when our trucker friend pulled to a stop.

"Well, I'll be damned!" He exclaimed. "I can't believe that a couple of women and a kid ever got that tire off. I really didn't think it would come off. How did you do it?"

As he finished tightening up the bolts for us, we explained how we had gotten the tire off. We also warned him to keep an eye out for that red car up ahead, with our intoxicated friend at the wheel. That guy shouldn't be driving, but we didn't have any way to stop him.

After that experience, it was sort of an anticlimax to hook onto the car with a chain, and tow it back into town. Of course, it had taken us much longer than we planned. It was nearly 12:30 a.m. when we met Ralph coming up the highway, looking for us. He had really been worried when we were not back by 10:00 p.m., so when he got off work at midnight, he came looking. We were all tickled that everything was finally going smoothly. I'm pretty sure I *had* said "don't worry," after all.

However, my plans had changed. Instead of leaving for the mine, I decided to spend the night (what was left of it) at North Pole. I got up early the next morning, got the Weps going and left for the mine. I had an uneventful trip, and, by some miracle I didn't forget the box of parts that were in the car.

I thought that Stan and the girls would be worried about what had happened to me, but they seemed to take my absence in stride. "I figured you'd eventually show up." Stan said. And I had, with that troublesome box.

Cyndi with Winona on the left and Vacca on the right

Chapter 28

As Far as He'd Go

Getting our menagerie to the mine presented some problems that spring of 1975. The previous year, we only had two horses, and rented a two-horse trailer. This year, however, we had added an additional horse to the two pigs, two ducks, two geese, and twenty-five chickens of our budding farm. School was out for the summer, and it was time to move to the mine.

We had already made several trips up the Elliott Highway to the mine that spring, and the road was really in bad condition. They were upgrading the Elliott Highway, since construction of the Trans-Alaska Pipeline was in full swing, and the Elliott Highway paralleled the pipeline corridor.

The construction company was in the process of hauling eighty-foot lengths of pipe to the North Slope, using "our" road. When the frost had gone out that spring, some trucks had found sink holes in several places on the Highway, creating huge mud holes. This kept the road repair crews busy trying to keep it passable.

"Hey," I called to Stan. "Look here in the paper. This guy is advertising a four-horse trailer for lease. Why not give him a call?"

After extensive negotiations, it was all settled. The guy with the horse trailer would come by our house at 4:00 a.m. next Saturday morning; we'd load the three horses, and be on our way by 4:30. By leaving so early, the guys figured we could take advantage of any frost that might remain from the overnight freezing temps to keep the mud holes stiffer, and we might be ahead of most of the traffic. The owner of the trailer would pull it with his one-ton truck, and he was convinced that we would have no trouble. It all sounded great. Someone *should* have said "don't worry!"

"What time do we have to start loading our other critters, so we'll be ready when the trailer gets here at 4:00 a.m.?" I asked Stan. "And, how can we get them all loaded in the Gray Ghost? We can't drive over to the barn, because the lawn is too soggy; we'd get stuck. Besides, we don't want to tear up the lawn."

"I have it all figured out," Stan replied. "I have this big wooden box that we'll put in the Gray Ghost for the pigs, and we can load the chickens into some cardboard boxes. I'll run down to the store and get the boxes for the chickens. We can put the ducks and geese into that large wire crate that we use for the rabbits. I think if we start about 3:00 a.m., we ought to be done by the time the horse trailer gets here. We'll just have to pack them all over to the van, but I think we can make the pigs walk."

I've heard it said that something impossible would happen when pigs fly, but pigs walk? I wondered, *is this a new way of saying that we can do the impossible?*

Off to the store he cheerfully went, and came home with a whole car-full of cardboard boxes. We cut holes in the boxes so the chickens would have lots of air, and piled them up near the van. Then, off to bed early, since we were going to be up before the crack of dawn.

So here we were at 3:00 a.m. on a Saturday morning, getting our chickens, ducks, geese, and pigs loaded into the Gray Ghost.

"The first thing we have to do is load the pigs," Stan said. "Here's what we'll do. I'll put these loops of rope over their front legs, so that way I can pick the front legs up off the ground and steer them. You follow along behind, and if they slow down, twist their tail a bit."

Twist their tail? Me? "You want me to twist their tail? That doesn't sound very nice." I gasped.

The first pig would not cooperate at all. He apparently thought that being rudely rousted from his nice warm bed at 3:00 a.m. was for the birds. So, he'd charge first one way, then the other. Stan's makeshift harness worked well, though, and before very long, we were racing across the lawn with the pig squealing at the top of his lungs. Every time he'd slow down, I'd give a little twist to his tail, and he'd squeal louder, but move. We finally got him to the Gray Ghost and heaved him into the wooden box. Then, back for the next one. This one wasn't nearly as vocal, but still loud enough to wake the dead (and no doubt the poor neighbors).

When they were both safely in the wooden box, I asked Stan, "What are you going to use for a lid?"

"Lid?" He looked perplexed. "Why do we need a lid? They're not going to jump out of there, and this way, they have plenty of air."

"Makes sense to me," I replied. "I guess we really don't need a lid."

Catching the chickens was easy. They were all sitting on their roosts, blinking their sleepy eyes. The only problem was that during the night, our boxes had gotten damp from the dew. However, they seemed to hold just fine, so we stacked them into the Grey Ghost, with between two and eight chickens per box, depending on the size of the box.

"Just room for the cage with the ducks and geese," Stan said. "Then, we only have the rabbit cage to fit in, and that ought to be easy."

We were just finishing-up loading the Gray Ghost when the horse trailer arrived. We brought all three horses over at the same time. Stormy's Vaquero (we called him "Vacca") and Goliath walked right up the ramp and into the trailer. Then it was

Winona's turn. She was our appaloosa filly, who was always a bit flighty, and one never knew what she would do next. In this instance, getting into the horse trailer wasn't her idea of an early morning jaunt, even though the other two horses were happily munching on hay in the trailer. No way was she going to get in there. Every time we'd lead her close to the ramp. She just planted her feet, snorted, looked at us with wild eyes, and then tried to take off for the barn.

"Give me that lead rope," Stan finally called. "You're not doing it right." He grabbed the lead rope, and low and behold, he had the same luck as the rest of us. She adamantly refused to get into the horse trailer. Coaxing with grain didn't work. And, the guy that owned the horse-trailer was getting antsy to be on the road.

"Put this rope around her hind quarters, and you can each pull on it, while I get up into the horse trailer and pull on her halter," Stan directed. So, we did. But, pull as hard as we could, we could not make her go into that trailer. I wondered, *what would happen if I twisted her tail?* But, I didn't offer.

The time was getting later and later. And still that horse refused to get into the trailer. Finally, Stan said, "Go get me a handkerchief." So, off I went to find a handkerchief. I questioned, *not sure why he feels the need for a handkerchief ... did he suddenly have an urge to blow his nose?* But, I didn't question him out-loud. I was surprised upon my return, when he didn't blow his nose with the handkerchief at all. He put it over Winona's eyes, and gently led her into the horse trailer, where she happily began munching on the hay with the other two horses.

The girls (Sue and Sal) rode with the guy in his truck, pulling the horse trailer. Stan, Cyndi, I, and our two dogs (a Labrador named Sam and our beagle Jeffrey) climbed into the front seat of the Gray Ghost. Talk about a close fit. Both dogs had to sit on the floor on our feet, or on a lap. We opted for the floor, but they wanted the laps. We managed to all get in and slam the doors shut. There was quite a din in the Ghost, what with the oinking of the pigs, the clucking of the chickens, an occasional crow from the rooster, and the honking of the geese. But, we were finally on the road, and it was only 5:30 a.m.

The first part of the trip went without a hitch, although we imagined seeing the lights come on in every home we passed as the occupants wondered what in the world was going through their neighborhood, making that raucous noise.

Then, things started going downhill. We were about forty miles from the cabin, when we heard a scrabbling sound in the back of the van, and noticed that some of the chickens had broken out of their damp boxes. They were perched on top of their boxes, instead of in them. It wasn't long before we got to the mud hole section of the road. That first mud hole was a doozy. The horse trailer nearly bogged down, and before our trucker friend got the trailer pulled through, it was scraping mud like a snowplow.

As we went through that first bumpy mud hole, one of the chickens fell off its box, let out a large squawk, and landed in the open box with the pigs. The pigs refused to take this insult laying down, so they tried to catch the chicken in their mouths, amid loud squeals and grunts. The chicken burst out of the box like she had a stick of dynamite tied to her, squawking at the top of her lungs, and leaving behind some nice feathers.

Of course, the dogs needed to see what was going on, and nearly crushed us in their effort to get back and help. We weren't sure if they wanted to help the chicken or the pigs. We finally got things calmed down and continued down the road.

However, there were several more mud holes, and each one seemed to be worse than the one before. We would have to take a big run for the mud hole, and would just barely make it through before we were slowed to a crawl. We were lucky that the one-ton truck pulling the horse trailer had four-wheel drive, as did the Gray Ghost.

Soon another chicken fell into the pig box, with the same results as before. I think the pigs began to enjoy themselves by this time, hoping they could have dinner on the go. And, the chickens were too stupid to know they were in mortal danger. We continued down the road, with the pigs trying for dinner again, and again. Before long we had so many feathers floating in the Gray Ghost, we could have made several pillows.

Just before we crossed the Tatalina River, the driver of the horse trailer pulled over into a wide parking area along the river. We figured he needed a break, and we certainly did, too. Being careful to get out of the Gray Ghost and leave all the chickens inside, we were really surprised when he said, "This is as far as I go. Any more of this road, and my trailer will be pulled apart. I'm afraid it might already have been damaged. You can just walk the horses the rest of the way. I asked the girls, and they said it's only about fifteen miles from here."

There was no changing his mind, so we off-loaded the horses. But, as more and more of the boxes were getting weak and discharging chickens, we needed to get to the mine and get them unloaded as quickly as possible. We couldn't possibly follow along with the walking horses. We wouldn't have a chicken left in a box.

"I tell you what," Stan said, "You stay with Sallie and Sue and ride the horses. Cyndi and I will go and get these chickens hauled across the river and put into the barn and get the pigs in their pen; then we'll come back and see how you're doing."

Getting the horses saddled and ready to ride was a big job, especially with Winona. She wasn't very happy about her trip in the horse trailer. She practically refused to let us saddle her. But, we finally got the job done (we almost had to resort to the old handkerchief trick again) and were ready for our adventure. None of the horses had exercised much since the long winter, but they were about to. Stan and Cyndi departed for the mine, we mounted the horses, and away we went. I rode Winona, since she was the flightiest. Sue rode Vacca, and Sallie rode Goliath.

We started off slowly, and it was very pleasant, except when a truck would pass. Winona thought a truck was a good excuse for going over the edge of the road, and taking off for parts unknown. But I managed—with major difficulty—to keep her under control, and we made our way slowly down the road towards home.

About an hour later, Stan and Cyndi returned in the Gray Ghost, bringing us a much-needed drink of water. By this time, we were convinced that Winona was about on her last legs. She had been fighting pneumonia most of the winter, and was blowing hard, looking wild eyed around at everything, and walking very slowly. In fact, we had started to lead the horses, since all three seemed to be getting very tired.

I was happy to see that Stan and Cyndi had successfully gotten all the loose chickens out of the Ghost, although the chickens had left behind quite a mess. They were not one bit housebroken and there were feathers everywhere.

"Do you think Cyndi could ride Winona?" Stan asked. "She's much lighter than you are."

"I don't know," I replied. "At times Winona acts very docile and then the next minute, she acts like a madman. Maybe Sue can ride Goliath, Sallie could ride Winona, and I can ride Vacca. But you know, at the rate we're going, it will take us three hours to get to the mine, and its lunch time. What can you do about that?"

"Well, I guess Cyndi and I could go back to the cabin, make you guys some sandwiches, and load the "Booney Bike" into the Ghost (the Booney Bike was a mechanized two-wheel contraption.) Then, we could leave the Ghost at the Tolovana River with the sandwiches, and I could ride home on the Booney Bike. I have lots of work that needs to be done, pronto. Cyndi can visit with the folks at the river until you get there, and then she can ride Goliath home, while you drive the Ghost."

"I don't have a spare key," I said. "How can you leave the Ghost unlocked at the river with the key in it, and not have someone steal it? Or what if someone steals our sandwiches?" I was getting hungry.

"I'll leave the key under the front seat," he replied, "And you can find it. I'm sure nobody will bother the Ghost sitting there. You know those folks are staying just across the river, I'm sure they'll keep their eye on it for us if I ask."

On down the road we continued. We had switched horses, and now Sallie oversaw Winona, I had Vacca, and Sue had Goliath. Sometimes we rode. But most of the time we led the horses, mainly because Winona was acting so tired.

We were very, very happy to see the campground on the Tolovana River. And, there sat the Gray Ghost, with a delicious lunch in it. We let the horses drink in the river, and then let them graze, while I went to find Cyndi. She had enjoyed her visit, but was happy to see me. We all sat at a picnic table and enjoyed our lunch until it was time to go. Not only had Stan made some delicious bologna sandwiches, but he'd even included some dill pickles. *Can you tell we were starved?* We tightened the cinches on the horses, and I went to find the key for the Ghost. Guess what? No key.

We looked and looked for the key, but could not find it. Finally, I walked across the bridge to where the folks were camped, and asked if perhaps Stan had left the key with them. "No," they replied.

Back across the river, I was wondering what to do when Sallie said, "Mom, while you were gone, I'm sure I saw someone over near the Ghost. I don't know what he was doing, but I'm sure it was a person."

Upon inspection, there lay the key under the seat where it was supposed to be. Either the unknown person had returned the key, or I'd been blind in the first place. We never did know which was true.

Down the road we went, with the girls on the horses in front, and me following along with my four-way lights flashing. The horses behaved well. Their break, with the fresh water, grass, and rest, seemed to have done them a world of good.

Once we reached our turn-off from the Highway, the horses realized they were nearly home, and made a miraculous recovery; in fact, the girls couldn't hold them back. They took off and raced all the way across the river, and into their corral. They beat me home by a good five minutes.

We were glad this trip was *over*.

Sallie on Booney Bike with Weps and Pete's House in Background

Winona peers out the barn door

Chapter 29

Turnabout is Fair Play

It was the first part of November 1975. During the winter months, when the Elliott Highway was frozen, it was vital that we haul our summer supply of fuel for our mining operation. During the summer months, the road was peppered with mud holes and soft spots. Besides, a heavy vehicle would just bog down on our access road, and often on the Elliott Highway as well. So, that nice November day, Stan and I decided that while the kids were in school, we'd make a quick trip to the mine with a load of fuel. We had our four-wheel drive weapons carrier (Weps), and a large trailer, and loaded them with fourteen empty barrels (six in the Weps, and eight in the trailer).

"Hey, isn't this moose season?" Stan asked, as we were getting ready to leave.

"Yep, it just started the first of November," I replied. "Have you got your rifle packed?"

"Not yet, but I'll get it for sure just in case." He said.

We stopped at the bulk plant, and filled our barrels. We had an uneventful, if slow, trip with our heavy load in the Weps and the trailer, until we neared the Tatalina River. As we came around a bend in the Highway, what did we see in the middle of the road, but a young bull moose, staring at us with what appeared to be a challenge in his eyes.

"Whoa!" Stan exclaimed. "I'll see if I can bring this outfit to a stop." This was nearly in the exact spot that we'd played "chicken" with that huge bull moose many years before. Stan managed to stop; set the brake; grab his rifle; loaded it; jump out the door and raced to get off the roadway. Fortunately, the moose was in no hurry, and about the time Stan got off the road, he sauntered off the road in the same direction. With one shot, we had dinner, and meat for the freezer. I guess sometimes things like that *do* happen during hunting season.

Our next big quandary was what to do with him. Stan had his hunting knife, but he hadn't thought to toss in a hatchet.

He cleaned the moose, but we didn't have any way to make this 500+ pound critter smaller, and even with the two of us, we could not deal with him as one large chunk of meat. However, Stan had his trusty come-along with us, to help in maneuvering the full barrels of diesel fuel ... so after some pondering and scratching of his head, he got the come-along hooked to the moose, and dragged him to the back of the trailer. It was no simple thing to get him hoisted onto the end gate of the trailer, but with a little ingenuity and just a few censored outbursts, there sat the moose as pretty as you please. Stan used the come-along to tie not only the moose, but the barrels together, and we continued our journey

We were only a couple of hours late in getting back to our home at North Pole. But, we had the diesel in place, and the moose ready to prepare for the freezer. We had a very full but rewarding day.

The road to Livengood, looking from our lookout

Chapter 30

Dragline Delivery

"I think I'll buy a dragline." Stan tossed into our conversation one morning. I've heard of "bolts from the blue," but this was my first encounter with one.

"What brought that on?" I asked. "We were talking about Sallie's basketball feats, and how she is doing so well, except for her shoulders, and you drop that bombshell?"

"I've been thinking about getting either a back hoe or a dragline to help with stacking tailings, and I found a dragline for sale. The guy needs to move it, and he's offered me a decent price. It just popped into my head. Sorry for changing the subject. Yes, I worry about Sallie's shoulders, I wonder if she needs surgery."

"You can't just toss out something like buying a dragline, and then go back to what we were talking about. Let's hear more about the dragline."

He proceeded to explain that it was a 2-yard Bucyrus-Erie. It had a 60-foot boom and was parked at a nearby pond. The guy that owned it had been dredging the pond and selling the gravel, but his lease had expired. He needed to get the dragline moved, and didn't have anywhere to move it. The upshot was that the next weekend, we were busily working to move a dragline.

When I first went to see the dragline, it looked huge to me. I felt like a midget. But, Stan was undaunted. At least, he didn't tell me not to worry!

"How in the world are you going to get something like that moved?" I asked.

"I know a guy that has a large wrecker, and he said he wouldn't charge much to come help." Stan replied.

On Saturday morning, Stan met his friend with the wrecker at the dragline site. They got the dragline boom lowered to the ground, the bucket off, and the boom unbolted. It ended up in three pieces. The low-boy truck arrived in the late afternoon, and they backed it up to a convenient pile of gravel to use as a loading ramp. The dragline barely made its way up the pile of gravel, but soon it was sitting on the truck, with part of its tracks hanging over the edge. They got the boom pieces loaded between the tracks, got the bucket loaded, and secured the load.

We left bright and early the next morning. I drove our red truck with a large sign, "Wide Load." Stan's friend with the wrecker brought up the rear, with a similar sign. The going was very slow, since it was springtime, and break-up had just occurred.

We arrived at the gravel pit adjacent to our access road in the early afternoon. The guys got the dragline off the low-boy truck, and the trucker headed for home. They soon had the boom and bucket back on the dragline.

Monday was a work day, so we left the dragline in the gravel pit until the next weekend. Another friend of Stan's was an experienced dragline operator. He would help the next weekend. As planned, we met Stan's friend at the dragline about 11 a.m., and soon the dragline was headed down the access road. We were lucky that it was springtime and the frost was shallow. As it was, the dragline sank in a few times, and Stan had to walk back to the mine to get the dozer to get it moving again.

By five p.m., the dragline was in its new home. Stan's friend left, after giving

Stan a lesson. We spent the night at the mine. But, Stan could not resist going to play with his new toy. I was cooking dinner, when he came back in the door, looking very dejected.

"What happened?" I asked

"Something went wrong, and the bucket dropped about thirty feet. When it stopped with a jerk, it bent the boom. I think it just bent one piece, so I can probably get another piece."

He did find a replacement part, adjusted the brakes, and the bucket never fell again.

Dragline staging area in gravel pit

Chapter 31

A Trucker Learns Some Manners

Construction of the Trans-Alaska Pipeline was into its third year in 1976. The road was in the process of being upgraded from a little country road to an industrial highway, but that process wasn't yet complete. It was definitely not ready to cope with the overly long and heavy loads it was being subjected to. Often, we'd encounter even-larger mud holes, soft-spots, and places where the trucks carrying the pipe took the whole road to go around a corner. It was not unusual for the trip to the mine to take us several hours longer than it had before the advent of the pipeline, while a wrecker was dispatched from Fairbanks to pull one of the trucks out of the ditch. Some of the wrecker companies were making fortunes, while the rest of us just had to wait patiently.

Most of the truck drivers hailed from states like Florida, Oklahoma, or Texas. They were not used to driving on gravel roads, with the ice, sleet, snow or muddy conditions offered by the Elliott Highway. We were convinced that their inexperience contributed to some of the problems encountered in hauling the pipe. But, of course, there were some truck drivers that were experienced with the type of conditions they encountered along the Highway, and they had little trouble.

We went to the mine on Friday night, which was our usual habit. Going up, we didn't reach the mine until nearly 3:00 a.m., because of a truck off in the ditch that had to be righted and retrieved. We were getting used to the long delays, and had come prepared with snacks, pillows, books, and games.

We worked all weekend packing pipes for our own (much smaller) proposed pipeline for the upcoming mining season. For the past several years, hauling pipes seemed to be the normal way of celebrating Mother's Day. I was trying to convince the family that there were other ways of celebrating, but to no avail. So, after an exhausting day of hauling pipes, and getting our pipeline nearly ready for use, we were headed home late on a Sunday.

It had been raining most of the day, off and on. We knew that the trip to town would probably be fraught with delays. We had just turned onto the Highway from our access road, and driven nearly half a mile, when we spotted a lengthy line of traffic, stopped in the road. Stan pulled the Red Truck (we'd traded the Ghost in for a 1975 four-wheel drive Ford Crew Cab pickup that we dubbed the "Red Truck") into the line behind a couple of big empty trucks. Soon, there was a long line of trucks, cars and pickups behind us as well.

"I think I'll go see what the hold-up is," Stan said, and he set off down the road, in the mud, with Sallie and Sue following. It wasn't long before they returned with the news that there was a truck in the ditch, and it had the road blocked, but that the wrecker ought to be along in thirty minutes or so.

We sat in the truck, and had some snacks. Soon, the driver's door on the truck in front of us opened, and a little, short guy with a big cowboy hat and boots crawled down. He brought a bottle of Windex and a roll of paper towels with him, and set about cleaning his windshield (which was probably a good idea). He climbed on the fender of that big truck, sprayed his windshield and proceeded to wipe it off with paper towels. Then, when finished with a towel, he'd toss it on the ground in the mud. It wasn't long before he had a hefty pile of paper towels on the ground.

"Mom, he shouldn't be throwing those towels on the ground." Sallie said.

"He'll probably pick them up when he gets done," I replied. "After all, he is so short, he has to climb up on the fenders to reach the windshield. He probably doesn't have any other place to put them."

Soon he finished with the driver's side, climbed down from the fender, and swaggered around to the passenger side of the truck. The same thing happened there. He squirted, wiped and tossed until he had a fairly large pile of paper towels on the ground on that side, too. Then, he stopped in front of the truck and cleaned his headlights (which was beyond doubt another good idea). However, imagine my surprise when he swaggered back to the driver's door and climbed into the cab, leaving behind those piles of paper towels on the ground.

"I'm going to go talk to him," Sallie said. "Come on, Sue!" And away they went.

"You shouldn't throw those towels on the ground and just leave them," Sallie shouted at him. He continued to stare through his sparkling clean windshield, without even looking at her.

"Hey, you, I'm talking to you!" She yelled. And he continued to stare out the window.

I was proud of the girls as they went around to the far side of the truck, and picked up the paper towels. Then, they came back to the driver's side of the truck, and gathered up all those paper towels. About the time they had the towels all gathered up, the line of traffic began to move.

"Don't litter in Alaska!" Sallie yelled. With that, both she and Sue scrubbed the pile of paper towels they had gathered in the mud, and flung them with deadly accuracy right into the middle of the driver's windshield. Both girls then made a beeline back to the pickup, amid a round of applause from other motorists waiting in the line behind us. Stan put the pickup in gear, stepped on the gas, and we passed the truck just as the little, short guy was stepping down, to begin his cleaning process all over.

"We better not let him catch us," I said, as we followed the line of traffic around the truck that had been pulled out of the ditch. "He might just run over us."

He never did catch us, and the next weekend, we looked carefully around to see if the paper towels had been thrown on the ground again. We didn't see them, so hoped that the trucker had learned that he ought not to litter in Alaska.

Completed Trans-Alaska Pipeline

Chapter 32

A Precarious Tow

By the year 1976 we were getting concerned about replacing parts that might wear out on our 1953 Weps. After all, it had turned into a Senior Citizen. And, weren't the manufactures only required to keep parts for twenty years? We would feel relieved if we could find some spare parts.

When we saw a weapons carrier listed in the July Army/Air Force Salvage sale sheet as not operable, we decided to check it out. It appeared to have quite a few parts that were interchangeable with our Weps, so we bid on it. As luck would have it, we were the high bidder, so it was ours. Since it wasn't running, the next problem was how to get it from Fairbanks to our cabin near Livengood, where we usually kept the Weps.

We had thirty days in which to remove it from the Salvage Yard. Stan started working on it right away, and worked on it for several days. He made sure that it had four aired-up tires, and that the brakes worked. He installed a battery, and got the lights working. He decided the only way to get it to the mine was to tow it behind our present Weps. The construction of the Trans-Alaska Pipeline was still underway, so the road was often clogged with heavy truck traffic. It could be a long, slow trip.

My brother Henry was still staying with us. I felt lucky that he was the one asked to help Stan, which gave me a reprieve. Bright and early one morning in August, they set off for the mine. The first unhappy discovery was that the brake fluid on the parts vehicle had leaked, which meant there were no brakes. And, adding more brake fluid didn't help … it just kept leaking out. (Stan's repair job was faulty!)

"Don't worry," Stan said to Henry. "We'll just put it in gear, and you can hold the clutch in with your foot. If you need to slow down or stop, you can let the clutch out."

Henry said, with dismay in his voice, "You want me to steer this thing all the way to the cabin with my foot on the clutch?"

Shaking his head, he obediently climbed behind the wheel.

"Yeah," Stan replied. "It'll only be three hours or so, and it isn't that hard holding down the clutch. Besides, you'll probably never need to slow down." They decided to use a fairly long chain for the tow chain, to give Henry more flexibility.

With a worried-looking Henry steering the parts vehicle, and Stan driving our Weps, they set off for the cabin. They had gone about ten miles, when the parts vehicle jumped out of gear. This left Henry with no way of slowing down, if needed … so on a nice, straight, and level stretch of the road, he blinked his lights to get Stan's attention.

He was quite surprised when Stan pulled to the side of the road, and stopped abruptly. Henry didn't want to plow into the back of the Weps, so he steered around it as best he could, until he came to the end of his chain. Imagine the look on Stan's face when the rig he was towing went zipping past him. The chain broke with a jerk, and soon Henry was free-wheeling down the road until he coasted to a stop.

"What happened?" Stan asked as he caught up with a shaking Henry and the stopped parts vehicle. "I couldn't believe it when you went flying by."

"Well, it jumped out of gear back a few miles, so I wanted you to slow down gradually," Henry replied, "but instead you came to a quick stop. What was I to do but pass you?"

They gathered up the pieces of the chain, and hooked the parts vehicle back to the Weps, and Stan drove much slower from then on. A safe trip was made, although the finish was quite a bit slower than the start had been.

Chapter 33

Delayed by the Truckers

Back in 1966, Stan and I had studied for and passed the test to get our Amateur ("Ham") Radio Licenses. We had installed an antenna farm at our place in North Pole. And since we were actively mining at our property near Livengood, we put up an antenna for eighty-meters there. There was no telephone or other means of communication between our mining operation and Fairbanks, so this radio communication was an invaluable asset for us when one of us was at the mine, and the other in North Pole. Even with present-day cell phones there is scanty service near the mine.

Sue, Sallie, Cyndi, and I moved back to the North Pole house in August of 1976. School had started, and the girls needed to attend, although they were not convinced of this. Stan remained at the mining operation, and on the weekends, the girls and I would commute. Stan and I had a schedule set-up on the ham radio, where we would make contact a couple of times a day, conditions permitting. On a Wednesday in early September, we met our regular schedule on the ham radio.

"How are things going at North Pole? Over," Stan asked.

"Just fine," I replied, "how are things there? Over."

"Well, I just shot a moose out in the flat," Stan replied. "I wonder if, after school, you and the girls could come help me drag it out to our road. I can use the little dozer, but I need to skirt the soft spots, and it's hard to see them from the dozer, over."

"You bet. We'll be there with bells on," I said, "and congratulations. It looks like we'll have the freezer full this winter, over."

I hurriedly packed some food to munch on for our anticipated three-hour trip, and as soon as the girls got off the bus, we were on the road. Unfortunately, we had to wait several times while wreckers retrieved another Haul Road truck loaded with eighty-foot sections of pipe from the ditch. We definitely did not arrive with bells on. By the time we got to our access road, it was several hours after we'd hoped to be there, and pitch dark.

As we were driving down our access road, Cyndi hollered, "What's that on the road?"

Our headlights had picked up a strange looking object. As we drew closer, we could see that it was Stan on his dozer, with the moose in tow behind. He had managed to elude all the soft spots on his own, and was safely on solid ground.

He stopped the cat, and came back to talk to us.

"I sure am glad to see you guys," he said. "I didn't know how I could get that moose across the river without getting it awfully wet. What took so long?"

"We ran into some of those darned trucks off in the ditch," I replied. "The Elliott is getting more and more difficult to drive on. Anyway, if you can get the moose into the gravel pit, I can put the lights on it while we get it cut into manageable pieces."

It was a relatively easy task to cut the moose into smaller chunks (since he had both a saw and hatchet this time), load it into our pickup, and haul it on to the cabin. The dozer didn't have any headlights, so

Stan was happy that we could light his way to the cabin.

We got the moose hung in the garage and were tempted to stay the night. However, Sallie had an important test the next morning, and didn't want to miss it. The girls and I got into our pickup and headed back to North Pole. It was after midnight when we arrived, but the girls had slept most of the way, so were bright eyed and bushy tailed when it came time to catch the bus the next morning. I, on the other hand, was a bit groggy. But, we were happy to have our winter meat aging, ready to be cut and wrapped later.

Cow moose in Beaver Pond

Chapter 34

Delivering the "New" Dozer

We had to buy another bulldozer. Ours had broken down, and it would cost more to repair it than to buy another one. At least, those were the facts that Stan convinced me were true. It didn't take him long to locate one he wanted. I wondered, *was the "breakdown" of the old one triggered by the knowledge of a newer one on the selling block?* Surely not.

Anyway, he had purchased this newer one, but it needed a "little work" before it was ready to be hauled to the mine. The "little work" turned out to take a long time (waiting for parts was the stated reason), and by the time the arrangements had been made to haul it to the mine, winter had arrived. One day in early December 1977, the dozer was finally ready for its trip to the mine.

The plan was that Stan would ride with the truck driver; they would off-load the dozer in the gravel pit near our access road. Then Stan would drive it to the cabin, light the fires, and warm up the house. The girls and I would leave immediately after school, cook dinner and spend the night. Sounded like a great plan, didn't it? Of course, this one was doomed for failure from its very start. To begin with, the day set for the haul dawned cold as blazes, with a light snow falling. It took Stan and the truck driver nearly an hour to get the dozer running and loaded on the lowboy truck. Then, because it was so cold (nearly minus 25°F), they decided to just let the dozer idle all the way to the gravel pit.

"Stan, do you think you'll have any trouble?" I asked. "Remember when we had the other dozer hauled to the mine? Curt was driving in front of the truck, and going down the hill from Wickersham Dome, the brakes went out on the low-boy, remember?"

"Of course, I remember," Stan said with a grin. "Curt said he heard the truck honking its horn, and he figured what had happened, so he floor-boarded that old van of his, and was really flying when he got to the bottom of the hill. The truck and dozer were hot on his heels!" Still laughing, he said, "don't worry, honey, nothing like that will happen to us this time." There were his famous words again.

The plan called for me to have the Red Truck all loaded and ready to go when the kids got home from school. "Mom, can't we have a sandwich or something to eat?" Cyndi asked, the minute they got off the bus. "We haven't had anything since lunch."

"Let me check your lunch pails," I replied, thinking *sometimes they leave goodies in them*. And, upon checking, I found they each had an apple. "You can eat your apples. We're going to have a delicious dinner when we get to the mine, and it shouldn't take us more than three hours to get there." I said.

I shoved each of them their apple to tide them over, and we all got into the truck. We were on the road by 4:00 p.m. This was according to the plan. Of course, the sun had been on its short orbit for some time, and it was pitch black by 4:30 p.m. As we drove along, we fantasized about the nice warm cabin, and the moose steak we planned to cook for dinner. We were nearly drooling. We should be there by 7:00 p.m.

There was nearly a foot of snow on the ground, and it had been—and still was—*cold*. Of course, I was always nervous about traveling when the roads were not bone dry. While the road was a little slippery, it wasn't bad, and we made good time. It was pitch black when we got to the gravel pit near where our access road left the Highway, and where they had expected to unload the dozer. Imagine our surprise to find that the State of Alaska had plowed a big berm of snow over the entrance to the gravel-pit. It wasn't passable, and there were no fresh tracks there.

As we came to our access road, we saw some lights further down the Elliott Highway, but from that distance, we couldn't tell what those strange lights originated from. Nobody lived anywhere near there. Surely, they were not made by Aliens.

I made the steep turn into our access road, and was surprised when the cable was still in place. Of course, it was very dark out, but I couldn't spot any new dozer tracks on our road. A dozer track isn't all that easy to disguise, even in the dark with a new snowfall.

"I don't think the dozer has been on our road," I told the kids, with a worried look on my face. "I wonder if those lights we saw down the road might be the guys with the dozer."

By this time, Cyndi was sleeping like a baby. Of course, that beat the noise she had been making previously, still wanting her dinner.

Backing up the hill to get onto the Highway was no easy task, but I finally made it; after about ten tries. As we drew closer to the lights, we could see that it was, indeed, the tractor-trailer with the dozer. But, the dozer was still on the trailer. No warm, cozy fire for us, only a cold house to welcome us, once we got there. And why was the dozer still on the truck?

That is the first question that popped out of my mouth when I got out of the truck. "The darned thing died on us," Stan explained. "We left it running, and it ran all the way here, but when we gave it some throttle to get it off the truck, it died. I think the diesel line froze. We've been trying to thaw it out, but don't have anything except matches and our warm hands to use to thaw with."

"Isn't your propane torch in the truck?" I asked.

"It sure is! Boy am I glad to see you," he replied.

Even with the propane torch, it took about thirty minutes before the dozer was once again running. It had to be spun on the flat-bed truck, and was unloaded over the side. The driver placed some large railroad ties down about where he figured the dozer would hit, and they just drove that big D8 off the side of the truck. That plan worked perfectly, and it wasn't long before we were on our way. The trucker had to continue down the road into the town of Livengood to turn around, but we were ready to go the other way, and get a fire going in the house.

We had nearly three-quarters of a mile to travel on the gravel highway, and I was deathly afraid of any oncoming traffic. The blade on the dozer was twelve feet across, and of course, the dozer didn't have any headlights. The best plan we could come up with was that I would drive behind the dozer, and hopefully light it up enough with the headlights of the truck, so that any oncoming drivers would realize something big and massive was on the road. After a couple of passing cars managed to stay on their own side of the road, I breathed a sigh of relief.

It was another relief when we finally negotiated the turn onto our access road. The dozer slid sideways for a short distance, which caused us some concern. But, we finally were through the cable. I continued to follow the dozer since, of course, once we turned off, there was no way to get around it. Stan enjoyed the benefit of the headlights from the truck, anyway. We had the heater turned up on high, and were toasty warm inside the truck, but we could see frost crystals forming on Stan's cap.

The next hurdle would be crossing the Tolovana River. It was completely frozen over, and I was relieved when the ice was strong enough to hold the dozer. Then, it was my turn to cross. When we were nearly in the middle of the river, we heard a loud "crack," then a thump, and we found ourselves sitting on the bottom of the river with our back wheels spinning. The ice and water surrounded us, and we could not have opened the doors if we had wanted to. We were in a tight-fitting hole in the ice.

I immediately shifted into four-wheel drive, but the pickup just sat there and spun all its wheels. I couldn't get out of the hole in the ice. "Good Grief!" I exclaimed. "Now what do we do?" I blinked my lights off and on, and this got Stan's attention. He stopped the dozer and walked back to see what the problem was.

"Put it in four-wheel drive!" he yelled from the bank of the river ... the dry, dry bank of the river, I couldn't help but notice.

"I already have it in four-wheel drive!" I yelled back.

"Well, can't you move?" He hollered.

"No, it just spins!" I replied.

"Well, just wait a minute, and I'll see if I have a chain."

Of course, waiting a minute was no problem for us. We had no way of going any place. In just a few minutes, he was back, but the news wasn't good.

"I'll have to hike to the cabin and find a chain," he yelled. "Just sit there and wait for me." Like I said, we were going nowhere fast. It was getting on towards 10:30 p.m., we were all hungry, and the kids were beginning to whimper. I felt like joining them in whimpering.

After a long time waiting, Stan finally showed up, dragging a chain behind him. He had stopped to put on rubber boots, which no doubt was a good idea. It didn't take him long before he had the chain hooked to us, and to the dozer. That dozer didn't even snort black smoke when it pulled us out of our hole in the river.

What a relief to see the cabin, with a welcoming light shining from its window. There was smoke pouring from both chimneys. Stan had not only put on his rubber boots, but he'd taken time to light both fires and the propane lights. While it wasn't quite toasty warm yet, the chill was off in the cabin, and it was surely comforting to be there. It was nearly midnight when we had our dinner of fried potatoes and moose steak. Surely no meal ever tasted better.

We spent that night, and the next night at the cabin, and were happy to see that the hole in the ice was frozen over when we left. We could drive safely across the river back to the Elliott Highway.

Stan was very proud of his new dozer

Chapter 35

An Even More Precarious Tow

The National Parent-Teachers' Association (PTA) Board meeting was being held in Chicago that year, and as president of the Alaska State PTA, I was supposed to attend the meeting. The reservations had been made for me to leave at 6:00 a.m. on a Monday morning in September 1978. The only hitch was that I had to pick up the tickets on Saturday afternoon from the travel agency. The agency would be closed on Sunday, and opened at 7:00 a.m. on Monday. This was long before the days of e-tickets or smart phones, so I needed the paper ticket.

Stan and I had a heated discussion about a trip to the mine that weekend. He insisted that we had to go *that weekend* and get the Weps. He wanted to put a new engine in it, and wanted to get it finished before the Weps was needed to push snow off our access road. We had gone to the State of Alaska, Division of Motor Vehicles, and gotten "occasional" license plates for the Weps. This meant that we were authorized to drive it on the highways, occasionally. And he had decided that this weekend was the time to try out our "occasional" plates.

I was going to be gone for a couple of weeks. And, knowing how the weather sometimes dumped snow in late September, I finally came around to accepting his reasoning for getting the Weps before I left. Besides, that way he would have a project while I was gone. However, I asked him, "Why can't we wait and get the Weps Saturday evening, after I get the tickets, and come home on Sunday? That ought to give you time enough to get it ready to travel."

He had replied, "We *have* to go up on Friday night after work. I told a guy that I'd be home on Sunday. Don't worry, I can get the Weps ready to travel on Friday night, and we'll be home in plenty of time for you to pick up your tickets Saturday."

With me worried nonetheless, we had no trouble on our way to the mine. However, when it came to fixing the brakes on the Weps, we ran into *big* trouble. He didn't have the right part, and finally ended up Jerry-rigging something. He didn't get it finished on Friday night as promised, although he even had me out there holding the flashlight while he worked. Still it wasn't fixed when it was time to get some sleep.

"Don't worry," he said. "I can finish up fast in the morning when it gets light, then we can load the spare engine in the back in no time at all, and if we leave here by 1:00 p.m., we can get to town in plenty of time so you can get your tickets." I just shook my head. There was his famous saying again.

He did get up before breakfast, and went to work on the brakes. Then, after breakfast, it was time to bleed the brakes. Have you ever bled brakes? While I am no expert on bleeding brakes, I learned that it can be a very slow process. I also learned my part of the job. I was to sit in the vehicle, and when the level of brake fluid in this little tank under the floorboards (accessed through a trap door with screws) dropped, I was to add more. In the meantime, I was to put my foot on the brake, and when he yelled "down," I was to push the brake pedal down slowly. Once it was all the way down, I was to yell, "down!"

(Very original, don't you think?) When he yelled "up," I was to pull the brake pedal up … sometimes this required putting the tip of my shoe under the pedal and pulling.

When it was up, I yelled, "up!" and the sequence began again. During this time, he was crawling around under the vehicle, apparently doing something that caused the level in the tank of brake fluid to drop quite quickly. It seemed like that process went on forever that day. I was itching to hit the road.

Finally, at nearly noon, he announced that we were ready to load the engine. Our parts vehicle had a spare engine, and all those spare parts were coming in handy. I was surprised when getting the engine loaded went quickly. However, by the time we had lunch, did the dishes, packed our stuff in the Red Truck, and were on the road, it *was* 1:00 p.m. This was according to the plan. Perhaps I didn't have to worry after all, but how do you stop worrying?

Stan was driving the Weps, and it was my job to follow him. I suggested that once we got on the road, I could just go into Fairbanks and pick up my tickets. But this suggestion met with a resounding

"No!" In a loud and slightly mean sounding tone of voice, he went on to say, "Something could go wrong with that engine, and you need to follow along to make sure I get there okay."

We started down the road at a slow turtle's pace of twenty-five miles per hour (thirty going downhill if we were lucky) and I was beginning to calculate the number of hours it would take us to do the seventy-two miles we had to go to get to town. I was sure he could go faster, but he seemed to have only a slow speed that day. When the Weps was our only vehicle for going to the mine, we used to travel at the superfast speed of thirty-five miles an hour. But, of course, that was nearly twenty years before, and I must admit that everything had aged since then, including us.

We had gone only about ten miles, when he began slowing down, and pulled to the side of the road. *He is going to let me go on ahead*, I thought to myself. Was I in for a surprise! "What's happening?" I asked, as I got out of the Red Truck. I was thinking that if my surmise was true, I could be in town easily by 3:00 p.m.

"Something's wrong." Stan said. "The engine just races and I can't put it into gear."

"Oh, no! That sounds like the clutch." I said, thinking of my experience with the car several years earlier.

"That's exactly what I think it is," he said. "Here, hold the emergency brake back, so it will keep the Weps on this hill, while I check something out."

The verdict was that the clutch had indeed gone bad. I suggested that we just tow the Weps back to the mine, and leave it until I got back from my trip. This suggestion also met with a resounding "No!" Nothing would do but that we hook it to the Red Truck, and I had to pull it to North Pole. By this time, it was nearly 2:00 p.m., and I was really getting nervous.

After a bit of scrambling around, the Weps was hooked to the Red Truck on a short chain. "Now, be careful." Stan cautioned. "I can't use the gears to slow down, and I'm not sure how long the brakes will continue working."

"I'll be careful," I responded. "But you must realize that if I don't get those tickets before 5:00 p.m., I won't be able to pick them up before my flight leaves on Monday morning. If I can't make that flight, I'll let the whole State of Alaska PTA down; Alaska will have no voice at the board meeting."

"Is that such a crime?" Stan snarled. He never was in a very good mood when I was on one of the four trips per year for those board meetings.

Off we went. It happened that the Highway Department was doing some maintenance work on parts of the Highway that day. They had a berm of gravel bladed into the middle of the road. While most of the time, this didn't present any problem, it made it interesting when passing cars. Sometimes we had to cross over the berm and drive along the skinny little lane they had bladed. This made for a lot of swerving from the towed vehicle.

However, it wasn't long before I was cruising. I could see Stan through the rear-view mirror, and he didn't look very happy. In fact, he looked downright angry. I could see his mouth working in what appeared to be an effort to yell at me. And, he kept pounding on the horn of the Weps. Of course, that horn hadn't worked in fifteen years. I decided that I'd just ignore him, unless he flashed his lights at me. Since there was no way to tell him of my decision, I just kept on going at a respectable speed, and he just kept following ... hollering and pounding and steering as we went down the road.

We were about twenty miles from town, when we came upon a guy standing by his broken- down vehicle. He was trying to flag us down, and since by then I had made up some time, I decided we had enough time to stop, and see if we could help. That was a mistake.

It took Stan at least ten minutes of red-faced yelling before he calmed down enough to agree that we ought to give the guy a ride to town. I wasn't surprised when the guy crawled into the Red Truck with me, instead of into the Weps with Stan. Nobody would want to ride with a madman.

We continued down the road, and since I had to make up for the time we had wasted in that needless argument, I probably pulled him a tad bit faster than I ought to (and I had forgotten to mention to him that if he wanted me to slow down or stop, he only needed to flash his lights). However, everything went well. We got to where the Highway turns off to town, and I pulled over to the side of the road. By the time Stan got out of the Weps to see what I was up to, I had him unhooked, and was headed back to the Red Truck. "I'll be back soon!" I yelled over my shoulder, and away I went.

I got to the travel agency with five minutes to spare. Then I dropped off our hitchhiker at a garage, and went back to pick up Stan. By this time, he had calmed down, and was into the "don't speak to me, and I won't speak to you," mode. We were both glad when we pulled into our driveway in North Pole all in one piece. He was finally speaking to me once again when I got home from my trip. But until the day he died, if I wanted to make him angry, all I had to do is mention that tow.

Red Truck with Sam's puppy Junior rolling in the grass

Chapter 36

Accident on Wickersham

"Brring. Brring." I quickly dried my hands on a dish towel, and raced to answer the phone.

"Hello?" I said, as I put the phone to my ear.

A man's voice on the phone asked, "Is this Rose?"

"Yes." I replied.

"Well, I'm a truck driver, and I wanted to tell you that your husband was in an accident. Don't worry, he wasn't hurt. I called the wrecker, and he ought to be home in just a couple of hours."

"What happened?" I asked.

"I'm not sure how it happened, but he rolled the pickup. Don't worry, though, he really isn't hurt."

"What wrecker did you call?" I asked.

"Big Bend Towing, you know, the one that has the BIG wrecker. But don't worry, he is just fine."

Don't worry? Those were the two most worthless words in the English language right about then. I paced the floors, and chewed off most of my fingernails. Stan had left that morning on a trip to the mine, with six barrels of diesel-fuel in the back of our Red Truck. For company, he had taken our beagle, Jeffrey. It was mid-December of 1978. The temperature was hovering around the zero-degree mark, and there was about two feet of snow on the ground. He expected the trip to take about eight hours, so I hadn't even begun to worry until that phone call. After the phone call, worry was my middle name.

Two hours passed, then three hours. I couldn't take the suspense any longer, so I dialed the Big Bend Towing number. "Hello," I said. "This is Mrs. Rybachek, and I understand that a wrecker went out on the Elliott Highway because my husband had been in an accident. Do you have any information about that?"

"Well, Ma'am," he said. "I do know we dispatched a wrecker out there, but he came back a couple of hours ago. He is out on another call right now."

"What did he do with my husband?" I was really getting worried now.

"I'm not sure, I didn't ask him. But if you'd like, I could see if I can raise him on the radio and find out. I'll call back."

I hate to wait for a telephone call. There is nothing more nerve wracking, is there? So, as I continued to pace the floor, waiting for the phone to ring, I got to thinking of all the bad things that might have happened. Maybe he had another accident on the way home. Maybe the truck was beyond repair, and the driver had hauled Stan to the hospital. Maybe. ...

"Brring!" The phone finally rang. "Hello!" I shouted into it.

"Ma'am, I did get hold of the wrecker driver. He said they pulled the truck out of the ditch, set it upright, and your husband decided to go on up the Highway."

"Go on up the Highway? How could he do that, if he'd just rolled the pickup?"

"I don't have any more information, Ma'am. That is all I know."

Time really dragged that day. I decided that busy hands would keep me from worrying, so I had that house spotless before long. Then, I decided to write some letters. I didn't want to tie up the phone, in case Stan or someone else called. This was before the invention of "Call Waiting."

As it grew dark, I kept jumping up and looking out the window, hoping against hope that I'd see lights turning into our driveway. My diligence was rewarded at around 10:00 p.m., when lights *did* turn in … and it was Stan in the Red Truck!

I quickly put on my coat and boots, and made a beeline over to where he had parked the truck. "Where have you been?" I shouted. "What happened?"

With a sheepish grin, he said, "Why are you asking that?"

"I got a call about ten this morning, saying that you'd rolled the truck, and ought to be home by noon. Here it is 10:00 p.m., and you are just rolling in. And you have the nerve to ask me why I'm asking?"

"Oh, that. Well, I did roll the truck. I was fighting with Jeffrey for my sandwich just before we got to Wickersham Dome, and the road turned. I didn't. When I realized what had happened, I tried to get back on the road, but it was too late. The back end of the truck slid into the ditch, and then the cab just went over the pickup box backwards. It landed on its top, and somewhere along the line, it must have picked up some snow that melted on the engine. I shut off the motor, but when the steam started rising, I was afraid it was gas dripping on the hot engine, and was afraid that it might explode and burn. So, I kicked out the driver's window, and crawled out. If I hadn't done that, there wouldn't be much damage at all to the pickup. See, I pushed the top of the cab back up, and all it has are those little wrinkles." (Later, Stan put some clearance lights in the wrinkles, and the wrinkles were difficult to notice.) He continued, "The only damage to me is where the propane tank in the front seat bounced off the roof, and landed on my knee. But I didn't know anyone would call you."

"You were driving, and trying to eat a sandwich? That makes no sense to me." I replied, still upset. "How is Jeffrey?"

"He was out the window right after me. He wasn't sure he wanted to get back in the truck, once the wrecker had it upright. I couldn't say I blamed him, but since the diesel fuel hadn't spilled, the wrecker got the barrels reloaded, and the only damage seemed to be to the window, so I just decided to go on up and unload the diesel. No sense in bringing it back to town."

"What about the window?" I asked. "Wasn't that a bit breezy?"

"You bet it was! I tried to keep my coat over the hole until I got to the mine, and there I got a piece of cardboard. It makes it hard to see out the side view mirror, but it was sure a lot warmer."

With a new window, the truck was nearly as good as new. Another experience on the Elliott Highway we could have done without.

Cyndi riding Goliath and Rose riding Winona.

Chapter 37

Goliath Drives the Horse Trailer

We had just finished a successful year at our mining operation by the middle of September 1979, and were moving our belongings back to Fairbanks. Our belongings included one cantankerous but lovable Morgan horse named Goliath. Goliath was in his twenties, and did love to eat. He had been a barrel racer in his younger years, and still ... once in a while ... could circle the barrels in near-record time. But, mostly he grazed and ate.

We hooked the horse trailer to the Red Truck, and enticed Goliath into the horse trailer by feeding him hands full of oats. Then, we finished loading our pickup. And, as we said goodbye to our cabin for the winter, we all had a sad feeling. Cyndi, Stan, and I, were all rather long-faced.

Some of the road to our cabin was now paved, but a lot of it was gravel ... the dust could get quite severe at times. This was one of those times, so it was a relief when we reached the pavement, about halfway to town. All was going smoothly, until Stan exclaimed, "What is *that*?" Cyndi and I looked around to see what he was talking about, only to see the horse trailer passing us on the left-hand side of the pickup, with a very worried looking Goliath staring out the window. He had even quit eating his hay.

Somehow the trailer had come unhitched, and apparently, we had forgotten to hook the safety chain. What a helpless feeling we had as he passed us. We were in an area of the road where there was a deep ditch on the left, and, of course, we were in our pickup on the right. We were lucky that the road soon started up a hill, which slowed the trailer, but there was a curve near the top ... would the horse trailer turn? Would it dive into the deep ditch? And, what if a car came around the corner? This did *not* look like a good situation, no matter what.

"Look!" Stan said. The horse trailer slowed just before the curve in the road, and slowly veered towards the ditch. And, no cars had come around the bend.

"How in the world could that happen?" Stan asked. For there was an old, overgrown approach, and the horse trailer went gently onto that, and jammed its tongue into the dirt bank. It did come to a stop rather suddenly, which put poor Goliath on his knees ... and when we unloaded him to get the trailer hooked back to the pickup, he was shaking. He even refused to munch on some succulent grass, so we knew he was in a state of shock. He really did *not* want to get back into the trailer, but eventually the sound of oats rattling in his bucket got him reloaded. We had an uneventful trip the rest of the way home. And, we made sure the safety chain was securely fastened.

Cyndi on a recovered Goliath

Chapter 38

Mom and the Chopper

It was August of 1980. My Dad had passed away in March of 1978, and Mom was spending the whole summer with us that year. We were at the mine, and her job was to cook for us and do odd jobs, such as feed the chickens and gather the eggs. Cyndi had gone fishing with Sallie for the week. So, it was just Stan, Mom, and me at the mine.

As was my habit, I was planning to check into a 5:00 p.m. net on my ham radio. I liked to check in, and chat with my friends in Fairbanks. That day, I was busy putting the finishing touches on a roast, and getting ready for my net. Mom graciously volunteered to go up the hill where we had Goliath picketed, and bring him down to the barn for the night. She and the dog left, and I was puttered around, waiting for five o'clock and net time.

As it got closer to 5:00 p.m., I went into the garage, and pulled the rope, starting the generator. The net went fine, and I was just getting ready to say goodbye to my friends, when Mom entered the house. She looked quite disheveled and was without her glasses. She never said a word, just very quietly headed for her bed.

"What happened to you?" I asked. She didn't say anything, just laid down on the bed. "Don't go away," I said to my buddy on the radio. "Something happened to Mom."

I quickly ran outside where Stan was fueling-up the dozer, and hollered for him to come into the house. He came in, took one look at Mom, and then asked her what had happened in a worried tone of voice. She looked at him, and said, "What happened? Where am I?" We knew for sure that something was dreadfully wrong.

Back to the radio, I explained to my friend that we didn't know what had happened, but Mom was definitely not all right. He said, "I'm with Army Search and Rescue. Let me see if I can get a helicopter out there, and we'll bring her into town." Soon he was back, and said that one could leave in about thirty minutes ... where could they land?

"Now, that's a good question. Probably the safest place is on the Elliott Highway," I said. "We can get out there with the truck, and leave the lights on. It will be just past the Tolovana River Bridge, at about Mile 60."

"Okay," he said. "They'll be there as soon as they can."

We shut the oven off, leaving the roast in, and got ourselves ready to go. We had an awful time getting Mom loaded into the truck. She was like a limp doll, but she just kept repeatedly asking, "What happened? Where am I?" Finally, she was in the truck, and we drove out to the Elliott. I rode with her in the back seat, to sort of steady her as we went. We found the wide spot in the road, left the truck running with the lights on and waited for the helicopter to arrive. And, soon it did.

They had room for me to ride along with her in the helicopter. Stan went back to the cabin; put the roast in the refrigerator; loaded up the dogs and then back to the Elliott Highway to follow us to the hospital.

When Mom and I arrived in the helicopter, they immediately took her into the Emergency Room. The doctors found that she had a broken clavicle, a large bruise on her head, and a concussion. This was my only trip from the mine to Fairbanks that was not on the Elliott, and I was very thankful for the helicopter. Stan and the dogs had a worried trip to Fairbanks, not knowing what was happening with Mom.

Later, we found her glasses near a large iron flower box we had in the front yard. We surmised that she had probably been leading the horse past that, when I'd started the generator. Most likely he had spooked, and knocked her into the flower box, causing her injuries. She must have put the horse in the corral before coming into the house, operating on auto-pilot. Ham radio had saved Mom a long ride along the Elliott to the hospital. She recovered nicely from her experience.

* * * *

I hope you enjoyed reading about our (mis)adventures along and near the intriguing Elliott Highway, spanning the first thirty or so years after its construction.

The Highway is still thriving, and to this day I'm still fascinated with it. It has been a learning experience to watch it grow from a dirt and gravel road, into a paved highway, with many of its more interesting curves and turns lost to "improvements." Many of you are familiar with The Elliott Highway from watching the hit TV series, "Ice Road Truckers." The Elliott Highway is the first part of the Ice Road, and is still being traveled. I know it continues to provide many exciting adventures for its travelers.

67545269R00143

Made in the USA
Lexington, KY
14 September 2017